PRAISE FOR *ANCIENT SECRETS TO PROJECT MANAGEMENT*

"Robert served as project manager on one of the most challenging design-build infrastructure projects in our state's and nation's history. Working together daily, over a period of years, I witnessed Robert embody the principles he describes in this book—*Ancient Secrets to Project Management*—with special emphasis on his technical excellence and empowered team leadership. His integrity, clarity, and commitment to excellence helped guide the project to its successful completion. Through the process, and under Robert's guidance, the project achieved several engineering firsts and set a new standard in project delivery. Thank you, Robert, for your professionalism and for exemplifying what collaborative leadership can accomplish with your encouraging book for the new era of project managers."

—Steve MacLennan, PE
Client Program Director, Executive Consultant at HKA Global

"*Ancient Secrets to Project Management* is like getting a toolbox full of real-world lessons from someone who's been there. It's smart, honest, and full of insights that hit home—on and off the job. Every project manager should give it a read."

—Jeff Lessman, PE
Professor of Project Management, Civil and Environmental Engineering Department, University of California, Berkeley
Former Executive Vice President of Shimmick Construction

"Robert Schraeder has written the rare kind of book that blends hard-earned professional experience with timeless wisdom. In *Ancient Secrets to Project Management*, Robert delivers not only tools for success in high-stakes, high-pressure environments but also a guide for maintaining your soul, your family, and your integrity along the way. Drawing from both modern project leadership and ancient biblical principles, Robert offers a deeply practical, heartfelt, and inspiring manual for anyone who wants to build more than just projects—he shows us how to build a life worth living. I'm proud to call Robert a friend, and I highly recommend this book to anyone who leads, builds, or bears responsibility."

—Alan M. Pott
CEO of Techno Coatings

"I wish I had this book earlier in my career—it's a valuable resource for anyone aspiring to become a resilient, thoughtful leader. As an instructor at Oregon State University focusing on engineering students' leadership and personal growth, I found *Ancient Secrets to Project Management* both refreshing and deeply relevant. Robert blends timeless wisdom with real-world project experience, offering practical guidance for young engineers seeking to lead with integrity and purpose."

—Hanna Hoffman, MEM
College of Engineering, School of Civil and Construction Engineering, Oregon State University

"Integrating lessons learned from decades of experience with guiding principles from wisdom literature, *Ancient Secrets to Project Management* provides valuable insights that will lead to wise, effective management practices. The personal examples bring to life the concepts shared in a way that makes the information easily understood and applied to daily life at work—a treasure chest of advice for long-term career and personal success!"

—Paul White, PhD
Best-Selling Coauthor of *The 5 Languages of Appreciation in the Workplace*
President, Appreciation at Work

"This book offers deep personal knowledge of project management, leadership, and the fundamental principles and beliefs that guide our thoughts, actions, and choices. As an ASCE Construction Institute Student Days program organizer, I can attest that this book will be valuable for many industry professionals, especially students pursuing a career in civil engineering or construction-related fields."

—Katerina Lachinova
Director, ASCE's Construction Institute

"*Ancient Secrets to Project Management* provides a wealth of practical information about project management and life management I would have loved to have had in my career. I recommend this book to all young engineers and leaders. There is not enough practical information out there about these important topics."

—Scott McNary, PE
Founder of McNary Bergeron & Johannesen
Former President of American Segmental Bridge Institute

"Project managers will immediately relate with Robert as he recounts the many challenges of project delivery. We nod our heads in affirmation at the difficulties and smile with satisfaction at the hard-driving work ethic, the DNA of successful project managers. But it is Robert's inspiration for the book that one takes to heart. Ancient wisdom from Psalms and Proverbs instructs us on how to address the relational and technical challenges we face leading people and managing projects."

—Sean Gamette, PE
Managing Director, Engineering Bureau, Port of Long Beach

"Robert provides authentic and meaningful insight into the construction process and how to enter into relationships with the entire project team (owner and contractor). His years of experience in the industry, patience with the process, and thoughtful approach to resolving conflict make this a book worth reading for anyone in the industry who wants to learn how to maximize the chances for a successful project. Robert's expertise, faith, and humor make this more than just a how-to-succeed-in-the-industry book. All of his advice can be applied to experiences in life as well."

—Melissa C. Lesmes
Partner, Pillsbury Winthrop Shaw Pittman LLP

"*Ancient Secrets to Project Management* is a powerful blend of practical leadership principles and timeless wisdom. Robert Schraeder distills years of experience into actionable insights that help professionals lead with confidence, integrity, and strategic foresight. Highly recommended for anyone looking to sharpen their leadership skills and build a thriving career."

—Thomas McLinden
President, Aldridge Electric

"How do you build a billion-dollar bridge in the fast pace of the twenty-first century? You follow ancient wisdom that Robert Schraeder says saved his life. In this book, he'll teach you how to successfully walk the same ancient path while living in today's real world."

—Greg Leith
CEO, Convene

"Written with engaging clarity, *Ancient Secrets to Project Management* provides time-proven instruction for managing projects and attaining a vibrant life. Robert employs vignettes of how he successfully overcame real-life obstacles on major construction projects and presents practical action guides for your use. Revealing techniques for organizing your project team, overcoming difficult personalities, mastering technical challenges, achieving financial goals, and more, *Ancient Secrets* is a valuable tool for improving management and living skills."

—Rick Mann
Senior Partner, Watt, Tieder, Hoffar, & Fitzgerald, LLP

"*Ancient Secrets to Project Management* offers practical, faith-rooted wisdom to help project managers navigate everyday challenges with clarity and integrity. It acknowledges that change—and change orders—are inevitable and emphasizes the importance of giving early, timely written notice to resolve disputes fairly. Robert's approach equips managers to lead with competence and character in high-pressure environments."

—Brian Manning, PE
CEO, mc² civil
Former President, ASCE's Construction Institute

"This book has great insights into project management, business, and life in general. It is filled with key business principles wrapped in ethics, moral values, and integrity. This is a must-read for all construction professionals regardless of age, experience, or education and should be considered as a course of study in construction management and engineering institutions."

—Andrew Gautreau
Vice President, AGI General Contracting

"Robert is a national thought leader in construction management and design-build projects. In *Ancient Secrets to Project Management*, he has brought a full measure of his expertise, commitment, and faith to a book of lasting value. Through decades in the field, I've witnessed how Robert has applied these principles of honesty, fairness, diligence, and respect—all deeply rooted in ancient biblical ethics—to create not only structures of concrete and steel but also communities of trust and purpose. Whether you're overseeing a skyscraper or managing an ambitious school expansion, the ethical framework presented here will help you build more than physical structures—it will help you build relation-ships, reputations, and obvious quality that can stand the test of time."

—Ernest C. Brown, Esq., PE
CEO, Project Neutral®

"*Ancient Secrets to Project Management* is a must-read for any leader. It will sharpen your abilities, enhance your success, and keep your life from spinning out of control in the midst of the pressures of lead-ership. The book is not simply secrets learned through experience but is rooted in wisdom derived from successful leaders of empires three millennia ago. Robert shares how these secrets sustained him through leading many multi-million-dollar projects. If you are not a project manager but lead any kind of organization, you will benefit deeply from reading this book. It is incredibly well-written and com-pelling in its presentation. You will have a hard time putting it down, and its stories and principles will echo in your mind and prompt you to deep self-reflection."

—Clinton E. Arnold, PhD
Research Professor of New Testament,
Former Dean, Talbot School of Theology, Biola University

"More than a guide—this must-read gem is a catalyst for transforma-tion. Packed with timeless wisdom and real-world insight, it empow-ers you to lead projects and people with clarity and confidence, avoid costly missteps, and thrive in your career and life."

—David Triepke
CEO, Universal Metro

"I learned early in my career that when someone with epic experi-ence and expertise speaks, I listen. So when Robert Schraeder wrote *Ancient Secrets to Project Management: How to Lead and Thrive in Your Professional and Personal Life,* I devoured it. Robert has successfully managed billion-dollar projects and understands the critical impor-tance of leading remarkable teams. You don't have to lead at Robert's level to have your leadership skills transformed by this book. If you manage or lead anything significant, his teaching principles and tech-niques have worked for thousands of years and still work today. Don't miss this opportunity to learn from the best."

—Phil Cooke, PhD
Founder, Cooke Media Group
Author of *Ideas on a Deadline: How to Be Creative when the Clock is Ticking*

Ancient Secrets

TO

PROJECT
MANAGEMENT

How to Lead and Thrive in Your
Professional and Personal Life

ROBERT M. SCHRAEDER, PE

EASTWARD
HILL

Published by Eastward Hill
Fullerton, California
SchraederSolutions.com

Cover Design by Liz Schreiter
Editing and Interior Design by My Writers' Connection

Library of Congress Control Number: 2025909076
Paperback ISBN: 979-8-9986310-0-9
eBook ISBN: 979-8-9986310-1-6

To my wife, Nancy, a true gift, the love of my life, and my partner in the great adventure God has set before us.

CONTENTS

CHAPTER 1

HOW ANCIENT WISDOM SAVED MY LIFE

Blessed is the one who finds wisdom, and the one who gets understanding. . . . Her ways are ways of pleasantness, and all her paths are peace. She is a tree of life to those who lay hold of her; those who hold her fast are called blessed.

PROVERBS 3:13,17–18

The largest project of my career—a billion-dollar cable-stayed structure in a major US port—would become the signature bridge of the region. I was project manager, and like many of the projects I had worked on before, it was plagued with problems: cost overruns, schedule delays, difficulty with subcontractors and suppliers, strained relationships with the client, and discord in the joint venture.

The members of the joint venture were very critical of the managing partner for whom I worked, and I found myself attacked by all parties while trying to manage my team and the project. I was spending 60 to 70 percent of my days managing conflict while trying to forge a path forward with solutions and compromises. Having worked on difficult projects before, I knew the toll the strain could take on my health, marriage, family, and career.

Sometimes in project management, you feel like a ten-year-old kid trying to build a sandcastle on the beach while the tide is coming in. At first, the waves roll in slowly. Then they come in bigger and faster. No matter how hard you work, you cannot stay ahead of the waves. But you are a hardworking, conscientious manager who doesn't want to fail, so you keep your head down and keep working. Then management wants more and more of your time to explain the losses in profit, the schedule delays, and the eroding relationship with your client or owner. While you meet with management, the waves keep coming in and continue to pound your sandcastle, putting you further behind schedule.

I know how that feels. Years ago, I took over as project manager on a $600 million transit project, which was behind schedule and had cost overruns and turmoil with the client. I was commuting by train to downtown Los Angeles and had to arrive at the train station every morning by 6:10 to get a parking spot. I slept an average of five hours a night and gained thirty-five pounds. While working to get the project back on track, I was living an out-of-balance life and unknowingly putting my health at risk.

My wife and kids caught a nasty flu. I started showing symptoms, but everything was so critical at work, and I didn't want to miss any meetings, so I took an antibiotic and kept going to the office. I was fine for a few days, but then while at work one morning, a wave of exhaustion came over me. I went home to rest and have no further recollection of anything after that until I woke up in the hospital several days later. I had come down with viral encephalitis, an inflammation of the brain caused by a virus. I had run myself down so much that I had no resistance to fight off the virus, so it attacked my central nervous system. While I was in the hospital, the neurologist told my poor wife that *if* I survived, I would never be the same. Many who have viral encephalitis have permanent brain damage and take months to recover and must relearn how to talk and function again in life. I was very fortunate that, after a month of recuperating, I experienced no permanent damage to my mental or physical capacities (at least none that I am aware of).

After this experience, I realized that if you bang your head against the wall for several years, the impact on your health is cumulative and detrimental. When I was younger, I could absorb the self-abuse. I prided myself on being responsible and overconscientious. But as I have grown older and hopefully wiser, I've had to realize that I can't continue to work this way if I want to stay alive and keep my wife and family.

THE NEUROLOGIST TOLD MY POOR WIFE THAT *IF* I SURVIVED, I WOULD NEVER BE THE SAME.

As you can imagine, when I began managing the construction of the billion-dollar cable-stayed bridge, my wife and I were both concerned I might end up in the hospital again. I had to make changes in how I managed projects and how I carried the load of building such a huge, complicated project. But what changes did I need to make? Was there another path I could take?

I noticed that most of my stress came from strained relationships and the inability to set proper emotional boundaries for work. Even though I would go home at night to have dinner with my wife and kids, I never mentally left the project at the jobsite. I would wake up every night between 2:00 and 3:00 a.m. mulling over problems I couldn't solve and then begin the day stressed and not refreshed.

What could I do to avoid having another overwhelming and troubled project destroy my life? I turned to the books of Proverbs and Psalms in the Bible and used them for inspiration and direction. Each morning, I would quiet myself and read one or two chapters to help me manage my stress and develop skills to deal with challenging processes and difficult people, forging a wise path to move the project forward. I remember hearing in high school that Billy Graham would read a chapter of Proverbs a day for wisdom to deal with people and five chapters of Psalms a day to keep his heart tender toward God. I thought if this worked for Billy Graham, I should try it.

This ancient wisdom literally saved my life and my project. The beautiful signature bridge was successfully built. I am grateful to have been involved in a project that enhances safety for the traveling public and is a huge benefit to the ports of Southern California and the nation, since 15 percent of all imports into the United States travel over this bridge.

I am also grateful for being mentored through the writings of those who managed projects, people, and the struggles of life centuries before me.

What are the ancient secrets I am referring to? It is what ancient cultures referred to as *wisdom*, which is also translated as *skillful living*. Even though the ancient peoples lived in an agrarian society without the benefits of the industrial and information revolutions that reshaped our world, they still desired to live good, productive lives and struggled with many of the same challenges we do today. In chapter one of Proverbs, the author, King Solomon, introduces the purpose of the book:

To know wisdom and instruction, to understand words of insight, to receive instruction in wise dealing, in righteousness, justice, and equity; to give prudence to the simple, knowledge and discretion to the youth. Let the wise hear and increase in learning, and the one who understands obtain guidance.

PROVERBS 1:2–5

These verses greatly resonated with me because I knew I needed insight, instruction in wise dealing, prudence, and guidance to manage and lead a difficult project with challenging people. So, I turned to those who walked the earth three thousand years before me when life was slower and people had the privilege of making observations on life, successful people, foolish people, and those who literally threw their lives away.

You may be a talented project manager with vast experience and success. But if you are not able to recruit the right team, properly delegate to those smarter than you, actively solve problems, work with difficult people, and stay active in learning new skills (all without becoming bitter), you will deplete your reserves and jeopardize the project. I know this may sound difficult, but as you will see from reading this book, you can successfully move your project forward without blowing up your team, your client, or yourself.

You may just be starting out as a manager, leading small $25,000 projects or million-dollar projects. No matter the size of the project, the skill set of management is the same. You can no longer do everything yourself, and you need to grow in your ability to manage people, subcontractors, vendors, engineers, owners, clients, and processes.

To better explore these ancient secrets and see how they can transform the way you manage projects and your life, I have divided this book into two sections:

Part 1—Successful Project Management
Part 2—Vibrant Personal Life

PART 1—SUCCESSFUL PROJECT MANAGEMENT

Managing projects is a complex process. So where do you start? In this section, I've broken down project management into key disciplines. You may be familiar with the topics of each chapter, but together we will explore best practices to be successful as gleaned from ancient wisdom.

Chapter 2—Excel in Technical Acumen. You cannot manage a project without technical expertise. You must thoroughly know the scope, schedule, and specifications of the project. Failure is guaranteed if you assume the specifications and design criteria from your last project are the same for your new project. Chapter 2 deals with how to be technically proficient and grow in your competencies by understanding your industry standards, developing technical mentors, and implementing best practices and tools.

Chapter 3—Lead Your Team. Depending on the size of the project, you are either the star player, the coach, the general manager, or the executive upstairs (to use a sports franchise analogy). The project is not about you but about recruiting, leading, and inspiring your team. Chapter 3 reviews the skills necessary to assemble and lead the right team so you greatly increase your odds of making the best decisions along the way. Wisdom provides the tools to recognize skills and personality types that will round out your team. The last person you need on your team is another person just like you.

> DEPENDING ON THE SIZE OF THE PROJECT, YOU ARE EITHER THE STAR PLAYER, THE COACH, THE GENERAL MANAGER, OR THE EXECUTIVE UPSTAIRS.

Chapter 4—Protect Your Scope and Margin. How do you control scope growth and manage the project you bid with a defined budget? You must know your scope and actively protect both the production and construction of the project and the schedule. This chapter explores how and when to put your clients, executives, or owners on notice of potential cost impacts without alienating your client. Many managers fall into the logical fallacy of a false choice: "I can either build a relationship with my client or protect my contractual rights." Chapter 4 will guide you on how to do both with integrity.

Chapter 5—Relationships Are Your Biggest Asset. I cannot overemphasize how important it is to stay in relationship with your customer or client even through conflict. You cannot become polarized and blow up the relationship just because you are angered by wrong behavior. The definition of successful project management is overcoming those who seek to hurt, delay, and impact your project. If project management were easy and a guaranteed success, you wouldn't have a job. Chapter 5 will provide the steps to develop the emotional intelligence necessary not only to preserve relationships but also to make deposits of trust and good faith with your client. You will need these deposits of trust when you require help resolving issues that are clearly the result of your team's mistakes.

Chapter 6—Know How to Negotiate. If you are a project manager, you will also need to learn how to negotiate change orders on your project. In my experience, managers either thrive in negotiating changes or avoid it because conflict makes them uncomfortable. Successful negotiation begins with the end in mind—what do you want to accomplish with the change order, and where do you need to be at the end of the day regarding final margin, schedule completion, and risk? I know several successful project managers who blew up their project by taking on open-ended risk in a change order because they were desperate for the revenue. You must always improve your risk position and narrow the definition of your scope through negotiating changes. This chapter walks through the steps of negotiation in a way that preserves your relational integrity while at the same time fulfilling your fiduciary responsibility to your company.

Chapter 7—Track Your Performance. You cannot successfully manage a project without tracking your progress, cost, and schedule. Your project never goes as planned, and you will need to jump sideways and adjust your means and methods, production, and schedule. In project management, you aren't fired for losing money but for *not knowing* that you're losing money. Wisdom will build the discipline and accountability you need to accurately track your project and report costs and revenue to management. Chapter 7 lays out steps to track your performance and remove impediments to recognizing poor results in a timely manner. You must develop the discipline to regularly track the performance of the project.

PART 2—VIBRANT PERSONAL LIFE

If you successfully manage projects, you will be rewarded with good pay and incentive bonuses, but you must be careful not to blow up your life through unwise, destructive behavior. It is rare to meet an extremely successful manager who also has a vibrant personal life. Part 2 addresses how to live with success and thrive in your personal life.

Chapter 8—Beware the Pitfalls and Snares of Success. The list of reasons people in my industry have broken families is long and sad: pornography, affairs, avarice, manipulating cost reports and revenue to increase bonuses, bitterness, and resentment. When you are emotionally weary and physically exhausted, you are even more prone to make damaging personal and professional decisions. Chapter 8 delineates these unwise destructive behaviors and provides ancient secrets on how to avoid them. Not much has changed over the last three to four thousand years—people still succumb to the same temptations.

Chapter 9—Create Long-Term Success. In addition to avoiding pitfalls, you want to build good boundaries and habits that lead to long-term personal and professional success. When you are young, you think you can overcome any obstacle and often sacrifice your spouse and family, believing you will have time later to fix those personal problems. As you grow older, you realize you don't have endless capacity and energy, and you can't rebuild what is lost. Chapter 9 provides coaching and insight on how to create long-term success.

Chapter 10—Instructions to Your Heart. Finally, there is a spiritual component to your life. You have a soul that feeds your ability to work and produce. Most of us don't care for our souls the way we should and often ignore the warnings until we reach a crisis. My health problems were a direct result of not caring for my soul. I took on all the problems myself and didn't share the load with God, friends, or my wife. Chapter 10 provides practical steps to nurture your spiritual life.

CHARTING THE PATH FORWARD

In my industry, after every meeting we clarify and assign action items and chart a path forward to build the project. At the end of each chapter, I have included key action items to assist you in charting a path forward on your project. I have great empathy for those leading projects, and I want to do anything I can to help make you successful in your project and life. That is why I wrote this book, so you can learn from my mistakes. (As we say in my industry, "You can go to school on me.") My hope is that you will gain wisdom and insight earlier in your career than I did.

My goal with this book is to provide you with a resource that not only helps keep you alive but helps you thrive in your work and personal life. I have many colleagues who have died young. I have others who have been successful in business but have broken families. And there are those who have become bitter in life because they gave their lives to work and projects and don't have much left to live for now that they are older. If you are young, come and observe and learn wisdom, prudence, and decision-making in your life. If you are a little longer in the tooth, it is not too late to start living a life of wisdom and bear the fruit in your professional and personal life.

> MY GOAL WITH THIS BOOK IS TO PROVIDE YOU WITH A RESOURCE THAT NOT ONLY HELPS KEEP YOU ALIVE BUT HELPS YOU THRIVE IN YOUR WORK AND PERSONAL LIFE.

Project management can be exciting, fulfilling work as you labor as a team to build and complete projects that you could never do on your own. My hope is that by reading this book you will gain wisdom to choose the right path to be successful and fulfilled in life. The opening verses of this chapter are full of promise and hope: "Blessed is the one who finds wisdom, and the one who gets understanding. . . . Her [Wisdom's] ways are ways of pleasantness, and all her paths are peace.

She is a tree of life to those who lay hold of her; those who hold her fast are called blessed." The fruit of a life of wisdom spills over from project management into all areas of your life.

HOW TO USE THIS BOOK

This book is a resource for project managers. If you are just starting out in project management, I suggest you read the book from beginning to end to build a foundation of knowledge for management and decision-making. Sometimes when we go straight to implementation without understanding the *why* behind how we manage projects, we can easily be led off course.

If you are a seasoned project manager with many scars from managing projects, you can use this book as a resource for a specific issue or an area where you need a shot in the arm. Pick a chapter or topic and read it now. Remember, though, that wisdom is cumulative and holistic. I encourage you to slow down the pace of your life and allow the entire book to speak to you. The key to making wise decisions is taking the time to see the whole picture so you act from a position of strength and not weakness.

I have included an appendix that provides a summary of the key action items from each chapter so you can apply the ancient secrets to your project. You can also find more detailed resources on my website: SchraederSolutions.com.

There is much to be learned as we make observations and intentionally decide which path to take. Many have gone before us and struggled with the same decisions and obstacles in life. We like to say that we don't want to reinvent the wheel but rather use the best practices developed by others that have proven effective over time. As we study these ancient secrets, we look back over three thousand years to proven truths on how to manage projects and people and live a wise life.

Now, let's go on a journey to explore together the *Ancient Secrets to Project Management*.

Part 1

SUCCESSFUL PROJECT MANAGEMENT

CHAPTER 2

EXCEL IN TECHNICAL ACUMEN

The beginning of wisdom is this: Get wisdom, and whatever you get, get insight. Prize her highly, and she will exalt you; she will honor you if you embrace her. She will place on your head a graceful garland; she will bestow on you a beautiful crown.

PROVERBS 4:7–9

My first exposure to working on large projects was building an $800 million, twenty-four-mile toll road in Southern California. I started out as a design manager and was responsible for approximately 2.5 miles of design for the toll road and mainline toll plaza. For the first time, I had to understand a huge amount of background information that informed the basis of design, which included a full bookcase of preliminary designs, design criteria, and specifications. Frankly, I was overwhelmed. I didn't think I could ever get up to speed on thousands of pages of documents and complete the design. Our client had been developing the project for years and had prepared the preliminary design. Now our team was contracted to complete the design and construct the project based on their preliminary plans, *which contained errors!* I hated attending meetings with the owner/client and his engineering consultants when I didn't know the basis of the design, and I was constantly reminded that they knew more than I did.

My drainage design manager summed up the dynamic with the owner well: "Dan wants you to come to his office and ask questions. Then, out of his great patience, he'll tell you how to design the project. But he won't tell you all at once. He wants you to come back again and again to let you know *he's* the expert."

After two months of interacting with the owner's design consultants, I realized that to succeed, I had to know the scope, contract, and design criteria better than my counterparts. I also figured out that the owner's consultants were just giving me their opinions, which could have been affected by what they had for lunch. These opinions were not based on the defined project scope and design criteria, and they usually increased our scope and cost. In other words, they wanted a bunch of stuff for free. It took our team six months to get up to speed, but once we did, we knew the contract and the project better than the owner's engineers.

> ## TO SUCCEED, I HAD TO KNOW THE SCOPE, CONTRACT, AND DESIGN CRITERIA BETTER THAN MY COUNTERPARTS.

The journey to technical excellence starts with humility and hunger. On the toll road project, I first had to admit that, regardless of past successes and experience, I was not technically up to speed for this project, and those sitting across the table were better prepared. They were not necessarily smarter; they just knew more. Next, I had to do a gut check to see if I had the desire to put in the work to understand a complex contract and digest thousands of pages of environmental and design reports and succeed. Once I decided to put in the work and learn from others, I was on my way to accomplishing the first step of successful project management—to excel in technical acumen.

HOW TO ACHIEVE TECHNICAL EXCELLENCE

"Apply your heart to instruction and your ear to words of knowledge" (Proverbs 23:12). The ancients knew that there was no shortcut to understanding, and they instructed us to put in the work to obtain knowledge. You must highly value technical knowledge to obtain it. On my first complex project, my goal was to know the project better than the owner so I could confidently attend meetings and complete the design according to the written design criteria. Frankly, my motivation for becoming technically excellent was fear—fear of not knowing the right path forward and fear of failure. I knew that if I were to succeed, I had no choice but to put in long hours to gain a thorough understanding of the contract, design criteria, and specifications.

How important is technical excellence to you? Do the habits in your life reflect that? How much time do you schedule in your calendar to invest in your technical capabilities? The time scheduled will reveal your priorities in life. Once you obtain technical excellence in your discipline as related to your project, this knowledge will never fail you; in fact, it will save you from making costly mistakes. Don't fall into the trap of thinking that you don't have time to plan the work before starting the work. You always have time to get the project right the first time. Abraham Lincoln said, "If I had eight hours to chop down a tree, I'd spend six sharpening my axe."

What motivates you to become technically excellent? I interviewed key leaders in several industries, and they have their own stories on what they did to achieve technical excellence. Allow me to introduce them to you: Mike works in the commercial financing industry and leads

> **YOU ALWAYS HAVE TIME TO GET THE PROJECT RIGHT THE FIRST TIME.**

his own company. Dan runs his own software company, developing apps for large high-end users. Michelle is a successful creative advertising and branding executive with her own firm. Greg has been both a prime contractor and a very successful subcontractor in the building industry.

Mike's road to technical proficiency began when he worked for a difficult executive who gloated about his superior knowledge of the industry because Mike would never do the number of financing deals he did. The executive used his experience and knowledge to keep Mike at a disadvantage and shamed him so he kept coming back to him for direction. Mike says, "From getting kicked in the teeth, I was motivated to become technically excellent." As a result, Mike dove into understanding every area of financing so he was above reproach in his technical knowledge. This comprehensive knowledge was the key ingredient to launching his own successful financing firm.

You, too, want to find your path to success, so ask yourself the following questions: How do I win this request for proposal (RFP) by outthinking the competition? What is the scope of work, and what are the design criteria and specifications? What are my source documents? How do I separate opinions from facts? What project am I managing, and what does success with this project look like?

Proverbs 14:23 states, "In all toil there is profit, but mere talk tends only to poverty." You must toil—that is work—to become technically excellent. There is no substitute for hard work to gain understanding. But be encouraged: You don't need to be brilliant to become technically excellent. There are many smarter people in your industry, but few who are willing to work. As Thomas Edison reportedly said, "Opportunity is missed by most people because it is dressed in overalls and looks like work."

You also need to begin with the end in mind. When my colleague Dan designs applications for smartphones or software for computers, his team must first decide what the final interface and dropdown menus will look like. Before they write a line of code, they determine what the end product will be and obtain buyoff from their client. If they don't begin with the end in mind, they will constantly be rewriting code and chasing errors. There is great discipline in first understanding what your end product is and obtaining approval from your clients or executives before starting the project.

Another humbling proverb is, "A fool takes no pleasure in understanding, but only in expressing his opinion" (Proverbs 18:2). I am amazed by how many engineers, managers, executives, and lawyers like to make grandiose statements to try to demonstrate their knowledge. They succumb to diarrhea of the mouth and relish making grand statements and conclusions. But it doesn't take long before they incriminate themselves with their words. This brings to mind a commonly quoted proverb, "Even a fool who keeps silent is considered wise; when he closes his lips, he is deemed intelligent" (Proverbs 17:28). There are many times it is best to keep your mouth shut if you don't know the answer or haven't read the materials that define the project. You can often be thought of as a contemplative genius if you just stay quiet.

> **YOU CAN OFTEN BE THOUGHT OF AS A CONTEMPLATIVE GENIUS IF YOU JUST STAY QUIET.**

My colleague Michelle, who works in marketing and branding, received no official training on how to become competent in her industry. As a naturally curious person, she refined her craft by doing the work. She studied what the big advertising firms were producing and compared her work product to theirs. She chose the best in her field and worked diligently to produce comparable or even better work. And she succeeded.

Like Michelle, stay curious and keep on learning as you go. Never stop growing technically or in your management skills. Observe what other successful people in your industry are doing and producing. Judge your work product by those who perform at a high level.

And don't just settle with having technical expertise in your area; commit to learning how cross disciplines can affect your results. To learn other disciplines, you must start with respect and humility. You can't be an expert in every area, but you need to understand how all of the cross disciplines in your project or product development affect the whole and are integrated into your project.

The wonderful part of gaining technical knowledge across multiple disciplines is that you start to see how one discipline affects another on the project. For example, in designing and constructing a light rail transit facility, the horizontal and vertical geometry of the transit line is the key deliverable to obtain approval early in the design. All other elements of the design and the project hang on this geometry, including the overhead catenary and electrical systems.

We were designing and constructing a light rail project in Salt Lake City for the 2002 Winter Olympics. That was a hard deadline that wouldn't move. My rail geometrician was a prima donna and believed his alignment controlled the project. But the new light rail line ran down the center of a major city street, and the budget and schedule didn't include a complete reconstruction of the roadway, so he had to closely coordinate with the roadway designer. He had to wait for the designer to complete the best-fit profile of the street and then accommodate his rail design to match the grades. Only then were we able to finalize the roadway and rail geometry. We ended up finishing the project ahead of schedule, and the rail geometrician admitted that to be successful he had to understand and coordinate with other disciplines.

So, how do you gain this key knowledge across multiple disciplines in your industry? With observation, research, commitment, and experience.

On some projects, you may have two technical authorities to satisfy, and you need to know who is holding the trump card for your project and which criteria to follow. To do this, you must be willing to encounter conflict early in the project to solve key problems that will occur in the future.

I have overseen transit projects that were managed by a construction authority but operated by a different county authority. On one such project, we knew we would have problems with startup and testing if we didn't engage the county operation's personnel and gain their approval. So, even though it wasn't required we worked closely with the county authority to gain their approval because they held the trump card for final acceptance.

Hockey players talk about developing a way to slow down the game in their minds so they can see where the puck is going and know where to pass it for scoring opportunities. This is the same once you gain technical expertise. The project slows down for you, and you can see the outcome of certain decisions and comments before they mature to bite you. You can then anticipate where the "puck" is going and make changes to affect positive outcomes for your project. But you must be willing to put in the time on the ice and humbly work to gain knowledge and wisdom.

> ONCE YOU GAIN TECHNICAL EXPERTISE, THE PROJECT SLOWS DOWN FOR YOU, AND YOU CAN SEE THE OUTCOME OF CERTAIN DECISIONS AND COMMENTS BEFORE THEY MATURE TO BITE YOU.

WHAT ARE YOUR INDUSTRY STANDARDS?

In each discipline of project management, there are industry standards. If you don't know what industry standards are used for your specific project, start asking other managers or engineers who have done similar work. You can also make use of industry organizations to determine the standards they have published, like the American Association of State Highway and Transportation Officials (AASHTO), American Society of Civil Engineers (ASCE), Federal Highway Administration

(FHWA), Federal Transit Administration (FTA), National Electric Code (NEC), *The Certified Lease & Finance Professionals' Handbook* (for commercial financing), and American Petroleum Institute (API). Don't just do internet searches; you must swallow your pride and ask others who have more experience than you what best industry standard they use on a regular basis. As the nineteenth-century British Prime Minister Benjamin Disraeli said, "The fool wonders; the wise man asks."

In heavy civil design-build projects, we usually design bridges from the top down but build them from the bottom up. All the work in complex projects is getting out of the ground, which means that our foundations must be designed and verified for conflicts with existing utilities, drainage, or foundations from old bridges. Geotechnical engineers, who design foundations, have their own set of vocabulary and acronyms. When working on the billion-dollar cable-stayed bridge, I refused to be intimidated by language I didn't understand, so I asked the geotechnical engineers multiple questions until I got a handle on the work to verify that they were moving forward.

After you determine the industry standards applicable to your specific project, you then must research what documents your client uses to define the design criteria, specifications, and scope. Most of the time these documents are provided to you by the client. But there are always other resources the client uses that they don't provide unless asked. So, humble yourself and ask questions of the client's engineers or representatives. Ask them how they developed the scope and the design criteria. Ask them if it was their client's preference or a third party's preference. You will be surprised by what you learn.

The commercial financing industry's technical standard is *The Certified Lease & Finance Professionals' Handbook*, which is used to certify lease professionals. This defines the four silos required for financing—sales, documentation, credit, and syndication. If you work in the financial industry, you may not need to completely understand each of these four areas, but you need to know what is involved in these key areas and how to develop your team's technical expertise to be successful. My colleague, Mike, didn't just rely on the CLFP Handbook; he wrote a manual to train his team in financing. If you really want to solidify your technical expertise, develop a seminar or a manual to train others.

Sometimes you can learn what your industry standards are by figuratively changing seats with the owner, client, or prime contractor. An owner or client generally knows what they want and how they want to be treated. But their legal counsel will advise them to be careful not to dictate how the work is done because they don't want the client to take on unnecessary financial risk. They want a competent contractor to execute the work according to the contract plans and specifications, but they don't want to take on the risk of directing the contractor's means and methods and then become responsible for any potential failure of the work. In multiple meetings with my client, I would say, "Sitting in your seat, I believe you want this." They would then confirm the unspoken expectations they had for the job, but it was my idea, so it minimized their risk. As a result, I built trust by giving the client what they wanted and not just what the technical provisions required.

My colleague Greg knew from literally changing seats that the standard technical approach to projects and industry specifications was not enough for success. Greg, who sat in the prime contractor's seat for many years, was often frustrated that subcontractors tended to act as if they worked in silos and didn't affect any other part of the project. Greg found that his greatest operational risk was not his self-performed work but his subcontractors' work and change orders. A few years ago, Greg became an executive and operations manager for one of his key subcontractors, and he determined to behave how he wanted subs to behave when he was the prime. He knew of the natural distrust between subcontractors and prime contractors. The subs think that the prime contractors will shop their numbers and use their estimates to negotiate with their competition. The primes assume the subs are gaming them and waiting to issue change orders for key scope they purposely excluded from their estimates and quotes. So, in this context and culture, Greg chose to intentionally build trust with the prime contractor by being an open book with his price, scope, and risk. He knew very well that the prime contractor could screw him by shopping his numbers and scope to other competitors.

Greg exposed himself to short-term risk in exchange for building long-term trust and relationships. As a result, Greg became the subcontractor his prime contractors trusted and believed in. The primes would list him even if his price was a little higher because they knew Greg would not be coming after them with requests for minor change orders. Greg built trust and grew his annual revenue from $25 million to $100 million. Greg's technical expertise came from his experience and treating others how he wanted to be treated.

My colleague Michelle never assumes she knows what her clients want. In fact, there are many occasions where her client doesn't know what they want and hasn't clearly articulated the scope of the project in their RFP. Over the years, Michelle has developed laser-focused questions to ask her clients to help them define their project. Even when she is competing against large advertising agencies, she shines technically and creatively and often wins the RFPs. Michelle tells me she wins by "out inquiring, out proposing, outpitching, and outbidding" the competition. Because of her great advantage in assisting the client to discover what they really want, she outdelivers after winning the proposal.

I have won many procurements and bids by gaining a thorough understanding of the scope of work that ended up significantly reducing our bid. This upfront work paid off by turning in a winning bid and then expedited a fast start after we were awarded the project. On one transit project, I was able to delete five miles of a bank of conduits because it wasn't in our scope. My design team was convinced it was in our scope, but this owner had broken up the project differently than other owners. We often bring our experience from past projects to new projects and assume they are similar. But most of the time there are significant differences in the scope of work and design criteria. I have also successfully negotiated many change orders with owners/

clients by clearly articulating why their comments on the design and the work in the field are extras and not designated as part of the scope of the project. Many project managers and contractors often do work for free because they don't know what their actual scope is and are not accurately tracking their costs against earned revenue.

> **MANY PROJECT MANAGERS AND CONTRACTORS OFTEN DO WORK FOR FREE BECAUSE THEY DON'T KNOW WHAT THEIR ACTUAL SCOPE IS.**

My friend Dan must define the technical standards for his apps. His company follows the steps in a defined process to develop artifacts—a wireframe, a functional requirement document, a products requirement document, and a business requirement document. These documents are then used to develop the app and ensure that one portion of the app design is not overemphasized to the detriment of another. Dan defines technical excellence as "the balancing of the tensions in developing one portion of the app over the other (graphic interface, user experience, business analysis, etc.)." This excellence comes from experience and careful analysis of past projects.

THE IMPORTANCE OF TECHNICAL MENTORS

On your project, who are the technical experts on your team? Over my many years as a designer and manager, I have learned that I need experts or technical mentors. Early in my career, I chose five people within my company to be my experts, and I would go to them with technical questions. They were happy to help and never said they didn't have time to talk to me. If you are early in your career, develop these technical experts now, and they will serve you for life. I can still remember specific conversations I had about sewer and water design with one of my unofficial mentors, Rick. I even chose as a mentor an engineer I didn't especially like who was great in hydrology and hydraulics design.

You must be the one to cultivate mentors. Your mentors will not pursue you.

Later in your career, you choose different mentors to round out your philosophy of management. You will want to choose someone in your organization who is best at identifying elements of risk. Who in your organization does a good job of developing merit arguments to win change orders? Who is best at building organizational charts and identifying key positions for successful project management? Who is an expert at cash flow management? Who knows how to mobilize resources (people and equipment)? As you manage projects, always seek mentors to assist you in your growth. The best time to grow as a manager is when you are hungry for knowledge and experience.

One mentor you must seek early in your project management career is one who understands cost and revenue. Most engineers and PMs confuse cost with revenue. This is a fatal flaw in project management that may cause you to be fired because you won't know you're losing money.

The profound quote that opens this chapter tells of the benefits of pursuing wisdom: "The beginning of wisdom is this: Get wisdom, and whatever you get, get insight. Prize her highly, and she will exalt you; she will honor you if you embrace her. She will place on your head a graceful garland; she will bestow on you a beautiful crown" (Proverbs 4:7–9). To get wisdom, you must first realize what you don't know and then seek this knowledge. Ask questions, be observant, and ask your technical experts and mentors what they would do. Take notes, write out a project management plan, and have other managers review it. Never be afraid to admit what you don't know—this is the beginning of wisdom.

You may be involved in a new startup industry and not have any mentors. But you can always find others to inspire you who have obtained excellence in their industry through refining their skills. My

> **NEVER BE AFRAID TO ADMIT WHAT YOU DON'T KNOW—THIS IS THE BEGINNING OF WISDOM.**

friend Dan seeks out and watches YouTubers who are great communicators and have a specific expertise in his industry. These YouTube influencers have sought to understand their discipline so deeply that they can communicate it simply. By watching others who have achieved technical excellence in communicating complex ideas, Dan then strives to do the same to keep his apps simple and elegant in their performance. Dan has also had to backfill his technical expertise by reading books on business and by joining a peer group of other business leaders to help round out his knowledge.

Demanding technical projects may require you to seek and obtain second opinions outside of your organization on the interpretation of key technical specifications or design criteria. While working on one project, we had a $120 million claim over the interpretation and application of *one sentence* in the design criteria. The owner's application of this sentence in the development of the design delayed the project for well over eighteen months. My team members and joint venture engineers understood how the owner had applied the sentence, and we wondered if there was validity to what the owner was doing. In other words, were we dirty and at fault for the delay?

We decided to retain an expert for an independent read of the specification. When we met with the expert, he presented a different application of the sentence based on the context of the section. The lights went on. Our initial understanding of the sentence was correct. We were not at fault.

Sometimes you're too close to the project. Get help when you are in trouble, and verify your technical position. Use your mentors to talk through your technical struggles and problems.

> **GET HELP WHEN YOU ARE IN TROUBLE AND VERIFY YOUR TECHNICAL POSITION.**

BEST PRACTICES AND TOOLS (TRICKS OF THE TRADE)

It can be challenging to strive to be technically excellent while completing a demanding project, so you need to identify tools and practices to help you manage your project efficiently.

One aspect of that challenge is how to efficiently deal with all the material relating to your project. The problem with the revolution in data storage is that we now expect people to remember vast amounts of information. Fortunately, there is software to help you manage this data and comb through databases. Find software in your industry that helps you manage the vast amounts of design criteria and specifications. It is so much easier to manage data and conduct searches for key words than it was fifteen years ago. Most of us are adept at either Bluebeam or Adobe Acrobat. (I prefer Bluebeam.) Get the version that allows you to scan and create searchable documents. Then compile your documents into a combined PDF and bookmark the document. You can also download PDFs of design criteria and specifications from many sources. Any time spent setting up your source documents will pay huge dividends on your project. I did this for my most recent project and shared it not only with my team but with the client as a tool to verify that we were all on the same page using the same technical criteria.

Complex contracts can be difficult to understand. I also use Bluebeam to compile the contracts and all the associated exhibits in a bookmarked, searchable PDF. I then print it out in booklet format, double-sided, in landscape, with two pages per sheet. I three-hole punch it and put it in a binder. I can then take it with me and even read it on a plane. This way I'm able to see four pages of the contract at a time and determine the flow of the arguments or restrictions in the contract. I can get lost in the specific details, otherwise, and I don't see the whole picture. I still use my electronic version to highlight and search for key words, but my first read is in print.

Finally, I must point out the great flexibility of Google Docs, which allows you to take all of your key information with you on whatever device you have as you travel. You can access Google Docs on your phone, tablet, computer, or even a colleague's device. Easy access to your data helps you be efficient and productive.

My colleague Michelle has written a baseline proposal she uses as the starting point for all her RFPs. Having the baseline proposal fresh and current in her Google Docs keeps her one step ahead of the competition in winning work.

One of the most important practices I have adopted is leading kickoff meetings with discipline managers after winning a project. I know many project managers who didn't discover fatal flaws in the design criteria they were using until they had completed 70 percent of the drawings. Many wasted a year or more and had to start over.

How do you avoid this mistake? Assume that your team and consultants are *not* experts, because they haven't yet spent the necessary time reading the specifications. What has worked best for me over the years is to develop a detailed agenda and conduct multiple day-long meetings to walk through the definition of the project, the design criteria, and the specifications for each discipline. This is a mutual learning session as you preview the project you are going to build.

Bring a key administrative person to the meeting to take meeting minutes and assign action items with names and due dates. This action item list can then be turned into the agenda for your weekly status meetings. Remember, you are beginning with the end in mind. You are answering the key questions: What is my project? How do I know when I am done? What does success look like in this project? Along the journey, your team will learn their criteria and scope and become better managers through their technical excellence.

CONCLUSION

Proverbs 19:20 says, "Listen to advice and accept instruction, that you may gain wisdom in the future." All the technical understanding you learn now will give you wisdom in the future. It is not just a short-term payoff for your project, but you will also take it with you throughout your career; therefore, make a commitment now to be technically excellent. A quotation attributed to Henry Ford sums it up well: "Genius is seldom recognized for what it is: a great capacity for hard work." Put in the work to find answers and learn to discern opinion from defined specifications and scope.

I won a $900 million project by paying attention to the scope of work and technical criteria, which reduced our bid by tens of millions of dollars. During the procurement, my prime designer kept trying to design the project the same way he had previous transit projects. This approach was adding millions of dollars of scope to the procurement that wasn't required by the RFP. I spent hours reviewing all the design criteria and interfaces between the facility and systems portions of the project. Only then was I able to convince the designer that a large majority of the systems work he proposed was not required for our project because the client had already given the scope away to others.

COMMIT TO BEING A LIFETIME LEARNER.

If you want to be successful in project management, then become excellent in your technical acumen. Commit to being a lifetime learner. "Get wisdom," and you will be respected for the remainder of your career, and when you speak, people will listen and follow your leadership.

KEY ACTION ITEMS

1. **Humbly Pursue Knowledge and Technical Excellence**—Ask questions, be observant, and ask your technical experts and mentors what they would do. Take notes, write out a project management plan, and have other managers review it. Never be afraid to admit what you don't know—this is the beginning of wisdom.

2. **Identify the Industry Standards for Your Project**—What does your client or owner specify? What do they use as a resource? What do your mentors use for standards? Assemble a list of design criteria

and specifications that define success for the project. If they do not exist, write them up and show them to your client.

3. **Define Your Project and Scope**—What is the scope of work, and what are the design criteria and specifications? What are your source documents? How do you separate opinions from facts? What is your project? How do you know when you're done? What does success look like in this project?

4. **Develop Mentors**—Make a list of technical, managerial, and financial areas in which you are deficient. Identify two experienced professionals for each of these areas and ask them to be your mentor. The one mentor you *must* have is the one who will teach you the difference between cost and revenue in project management.

5. **Move Forward Confidently**—You have what it takes to be successful. Put your head down and work without complaining. All the technical expertise you obtain will be part of you for the rest of your career.

CHAPTER 3

LEAD YOUR TEAM

Whoever walks with the wise becomes wise, but the companion of fools will suffer harm.

PROVERBS 13:20

My best memories of managing projects are from being part of a great team and enjoying working with wonderfully talented people who were also very entertaining and often had quirky personalities. Harry was a talented claims and engineering manager. Once after we presented our claim to a dispute review board, Tom, the construction manager, asked Harry if we were going to win. Harry said he doubted it, and Tom, who was a very aggressive personality, berated him with many f-bombs for his negative attitude. Harry matched Tom's intensity, declaring we were going to lose because nobody listened to him and the boss's incompetent lawyer should never have presented the claim. If Tom wanted to win, he had to get off his ass and do something worthwhile. Harry then concluded with one final wish about what Tom could do with certain body parts. After witnessing this exchange, I thought to myself, *I want to work with Harry, not just for his great mind, but for his entertaining dialogue.*

So, who should be on your team? As a project manager, it is your job to recruit the right mix of people. Proverbs 26:12 says, "Do you see a man who is wise in his own eyes? There is more hope for a fool than for him." No single person can know everything required for the successful execution of a project. It is impossible for one project manager, no matter how talented and experienced, to know everything in detail. You must complement your knowledge with that of others who are better than you.

> ## NO SINGLE PERSON CAN KNOW EVERYTHING REQUIRED FOR THE SUCCESSFUL EXECUTION OF A PROJECT.

But what type of team members do you need? As the opening verse of this chapter states, "Whoever walks with the wise becomes wise." You must know what you don't know and find people who can help. Recruit and build team members who have a better and different skill set than you. This will both benefit the project and your own growth.

In this chapter, we will discuss the organization you need to create for your project and how to manage and delegate to your direct reports. Next, we'll look at how to recruit the right level of managers for your project that are a good fit for your team. Then we will address the culture you should develop to help your team make good decisions and solve problems. Finally, we will discuss how to envision and encourage your team for success and the necessity of celebrating victories as a means of building your vision.

WHAT ORGANIZATION DO YOU NEED TO CREATE?

Here are the first questions to answer:

1. How big is your project?
2. How aggressive is the schedule?
3. How fast will you burn through your budget when executing the project? (What is your burn rate?)

Once you answer these questions, you can begin to identify how big a team you will need and what your organizational chart will look like.

Functional Reports—How do you divide up the technical disciplines in your industry? In heavy civil construction, for example, here's how we divide the disciplines:

- Roadway/Civil (grading, paving, curb and gutter, barriers, and drainage)
- Structures (bridges and walls)
- Traffic (signing, striping, and maintenance of traffic)
- Electrical and Communication
- Wet Utilities (water, sewer, and gas)
- Third-Party Dry Utility Relocations (power and communication)

Across all these disciplines is geotechnical design.

After dividing up the disciplines, you may need to divide up the project geographically with multiple project managers to stay on top of the work, depending on the size of the project.

In building projects, we have a Rule of 5, which tells us how many foremen, superintendents, and managers we need to build the project. Following the Rule of 5, we know a foreman can only successfully manage five crews, and a superintendent only has time to effectively manage five foremen; likewise, a construction manager should only manage five superintendents. After years of managing large, complex projects, we've learned that a person only has the capacity to manage and lead five direct reports. This also applies to you, the project manager. If you have a very flat organization with all leaders reporting to you, you will fail in your oversight of production, costs, revenue, quality, and schedule. The key is to build an organizational chart that fits the size of your project.

> **IN BUILDING PROJECTS, WE HAVE A RULE OF 5.**

Below is an example of a simple organizational chart to manage a project (see Figure 3.1). The **office manager** or **project controls specialist** oversees correspondence, produces cost reports, procures small tools and supplies, and signs up the new craft labor. The **office engineer** prepares and processes all project submittals that need to be made to the owner and any subcontractor/vendor submittals that need to be reviewed and approved. The **project engineer** can do this on smaller projects. The project engineer directly supports the **superintendent** in planning and executing the work. They are in charge of updating the schedule and entering correct cost codes for labor, materials, subcontractors, and equipment. They also update the quantity of work performed each month and prepare the monthly invoice. If the project does not involve a majority of self-performed work, then the project engineer will report directly to the **project manager**.

The superintendent is directly responsible for all construction work and manages the **foremen,** who then direct the labor for the work. A good superintendent is usually planning the work two to three months in advance, while the foremen plan the work two to three weeks in advance. As you can see, an organizational chart outlines the roles, responsibilities, and reporting relationships for the project.

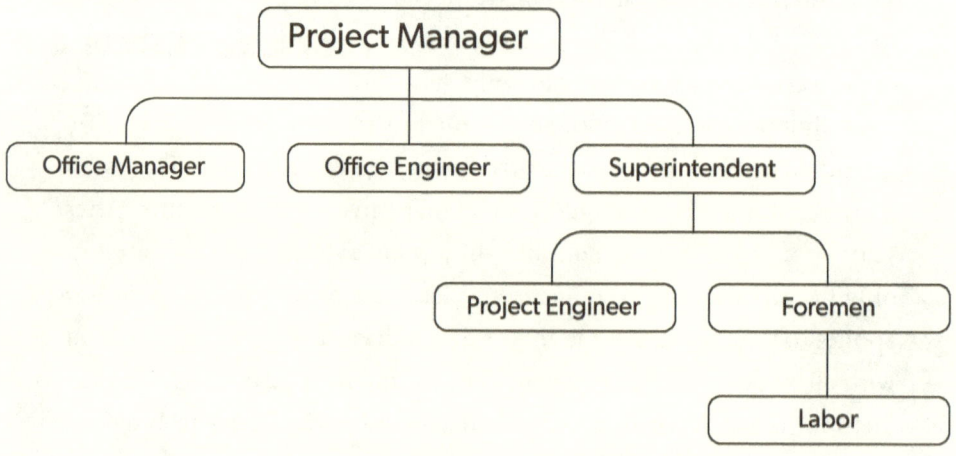

Figure 3.1

Determining Your Direct Reports—To determine your direct reports, ask yourself what disciplines carry the critical path for completing the project. What single technical discipline has the potential to blow up your project? What technical issue can consume all the extra time (float) in your schedule? What item needs early buy-in from your client before you continue to develop your project? The answers to these questions reveal who on your team must have daily or weekly face-to-face coordination with you.

You also may need to dive into the technical details for these critical disciplines since they pose the biggest risk to your project. On my complex multidiscipline projects, the biggest risk was usually geotechnical design and/or geometry design for bridges, highways, or rail lines. All other elements of the design hung on these disciplines. As a result, I made sure I understood the scope, design criteria, and specifications for these elements and then closely coordinated with the manager in charge of this work to ensure we started well.

Coordinating Across Disciplines—Similar to the project-wide risk posed by geotechnical design, there are some technical issues that affect all other elements of the design or execution of your project. In constructing roads, we often run into problems with the drainage inlets not matching the grading. We solved this problem by placing the drainage designers in the same pod of cubicles as the roadway designers so they would coordinate their work.

For your project to be successful, you must coordinate across disciplines to help your managers understand how their work is affected by other disciplines on your team.

Reporting with Clear Authority and Responsibility—After defining the organizational structure, the next task is to give your leaders the authority to carry out the work. Many managers complain that they are given the responsibility but not the authority to do their work. If you want accurate data on costs, production, and schedule, you must let your managers have the authority to execute their work. You can then hold them responsible for meeting the project goals for schedule and profit.

I hold quarterly forecast review meetings with my construction manager and discipline managers. We will meet for two days to review production, costs, claims, outstanding invoices, and their projections going forward. In these meetings, I include my deputy project manager, controller, office engineer, and claims manager so we are all on the same page. Every discipline manager is responsible for their work. When the work is costing more than projected, we check to see if it is a production problem or a scope problem. If it is a scope issue, and we are doing work outside our contract, we confirm we have filed a notice to the owner and are tracking the costs with a separate cost code.

I was on a job where the project manager, after reviewing the cost report with a discipline manager, would adjust the cost report and forecast without telling the discipline manager. What effect do you think this had on the discipline managers? The cost report and production rates were no longer theirs, so they took no responsibility for costs expended or for meeting the production forecast rates. What do you think happened with the costs and production? Costs went up and production went down.

As project manager, you must stay in your lane and let your discipline managers take responsibility for their portion of the project, their production rates, and their schedule. If you take it as yours, you will have a complete mess on your hands. Proverbs 20:6 asks, "A faithful man who can find?" Pick people on your team who are faithful, who will follow through, and who do what they say they will do. Make your managers accountable and responsible for their work so they will be faithful to execute the work.

> **YOU MUST STAY IN YOUR LANE AND LET YOUR DISCIPLINE MANAGERS TAKE RESPONSIBILITY FOR THEIR PORTION OF THE PROJECT.**

And if they don't execute the work, it will become clear that you need to make a change in personnel.

Identifying Managers Who Need Attention—In project management, you build your schedule during procurement to verify you have the proper amount of time to deliver the project to your client. You never want to overpromise and underdeliver, but rather underpromise and overdeliver. You can only do this by understanding how each discipline affects your overall schedule. Ask yourself what part of the project you are going to deliver first to your client. What is the longest duration of time to complete an item in your schedule? (What is your critical path?) There are some managers who are capable but cannot get closure due to the processes within their discipline. Lean into your experience. Identify what delayed previous projects to determine which key discipline managers you will closely coordinate with at each phase of the project.

On transit projects, the critical path technical issue that has the biggest potential to delay a project is systems design (train control, communications, signaling, SCADA, etc.). The systems engineers never seem to want to decide on the best path forward but continue to provide various options for how to proceed. As project manager, I had to insert myself into their conversations and research to force them to decide how to move forward so we would have time to complete long-term procurements for the project.

As I mentioned in the previous chapter, I managed a transit design-build project in Salt Lake City that needed to be operational for the 2002 Olympics. My systems design firm was out of Boston, and multiple weeks went by during which all they did was write white papers on train control and what was available in the industry. During this time, the owner and the federal government were getting nervous about the schedule. They would send thirty people to all-day meetings to review our progress on the project. I didn't know a thing about systems engineering, but I sensed it was becoming the critical path of the job. What was my solution? I made myself an irritating manager and demanded that the systems team meet with me weekly in person until they decided on a path forward and completed conceptual train control design. Once they were held accountable with weekly action items, progress was made.

HOW TO DELEGATE

Now that you have your functional reports decided upon and a clear organizational structure for completing your project, you must delegate tasks. As managers who excel in technical acumen, we are likely to fall into the trap of answering questions from our direct reports. We like demonstrating our knowledge, and it is easy to provide answers. Or maybe we don't want to fully delegate issues to our discipline managers so we can take credit for the completed work. In reality, your managers most likely know the answers to the questions they are asking, and they may do a better job completing the task than you. The problem is that we have taught them to come to us before making a decision and choosing a path forward. So, next time a direct report asks you a question, ask them what they recommend.

A funny thing happens with some direct reports. When you ask them to take care of an item, they may assign you a piece of their action item and wait for you to finish their task. Or a manager may come into your office and say, "We have a problem." By stating this, he asserts that the problem is equally shared between you and him, even though it's his responsibility to execute his scope of work. He just made you an equal participant in his problem.

"Management Time: Who's Got the Monkey?"[1] is one of *Harvard Business Review's* best-selling reprints. In the article, the authors—William Oncken Jr. and Donald Wass—describe delegating tasks as passing a monkey to a subordinate. For example, you may want options on how to reduce costs in building a wall. Your manager then writes up four options, emails them to you, and asks you to let him know when you can talk. As the project manager, the monkey is now on your back.

If all decisions are going through you, then you become the critical path of the project. The reason the article is so popular is that it deals with a major problem all managers face: how to delegate and leave the monkey with its proper owner.

The questions you must ask yourself are as follows: How much initiative do you want your direct reports to take? Do you want to control their work because you are the only one who can do it correctly? Do you want them to run completely on their own and then report to you what they've done? In their article, Oncken and Wass describe the five rules for the care and feeding of monkeys (which metaphorically refer to tasks):

Rule 1—Monkeys should be fed or shot; otherwise, they will waste your time analyzing what went wrong.

Rule 2—The monkey population should be kept below the maximum number the manager has time to feed. It shouldn't take more than fifteen minutes to feed a properly maintained monkey.

Rule 3—Monkeys should be fed by appointment only. Make an appointment and discuss the task. The manager should not have to hunt down starving monkeys and feed them.

Rule 4—Monkeys should be fed face-to-face or by telephone, but never by text or email. Be very careful with taking on tasks from your subordinate's emails. Make sure that your manager leaves with the monkey on his back. He has the action item, not you.

Rule 5—Every monkey should have an assigned next feeding time and degree of initiative; otherwise, the monkey will either starve to death or wind up on the manager's back.[2]

So, what does the proper care of monkeys or tasks look like? Have regular meetings with your managers to review what specific tasks you have delegated to them. Do not let the meeting end with the manager waiting for you to complete a task or review a document. Decide together in the meeting the next steps the manager should take to resolve the issue. The manager should always be assigned the key action item and should leave the meeting knowing they have the monkey. It is better to empower your managers to take the initiative and run with the solutions, but they may not be equipped to do the task required of them. In that case, you will need to train and develop them to think through the issues. The best way to do this is to ask questions.

I had a contracts manager who always wanted me to point her to the correct portion of the contract for merit arguments. When I answered her questions, I was providing incorrect training and, in reality, reporting to her. When I told her the answers and what to write, I felt good about my technical competence, but I wasn't helping her, myself, or the project. I needed to keep the monkey on *her* back and not do her tasks for her. Fortunately, as time went by, she developed the ability to read contracts and write letters for changes, so I did not have to make a change in that position.

> **MAKE SURE THAT YOUR MANAGER LEAVES WITH THE MONKEY ON HIS BACK.**

Every time a manager comes to you with an issue or question, refrain from automatically providing the answer or solution. Your first response should be, "What does the contract require?" If they don't have an answer, you may have a problem with that manager. By asking that question, you are instructing your managers in basic project management—knowing their scope. Before they come and ask you a question again, they will think to themselves, *I better know my scope and specifications before I talk to the PM.*

Even with good, talented people on your team, you will need to lead, train, empower, and direct them until they grow in competence, confidence, and a willingness to take the initiative. This process can be messy. Proverbs 14:4 says, "Where there are no oxen, the manger is clean, but abundant crops come by the strength of the ox." When you have strong, talented people as part of your team, you will have messes to deal with. Realize this is your job as project manager, to manage and lead your "oxen" to build your project. At times they may be difficult to deal with, but, as the proverb says, they will produce.

I worked on a $240 million highway project in South Carolina. The design team had decided to divide the twenty miles of new highway into eleven sections and then further divide the design into nine offices across the country. During the first three months of design, the nine design managers missed every submittal date per the schedule. Organizationally, the design managers for each section clearly had the responsibility and authority to complete their design, but it wasn't getting done. I told my construction design manager to go on a road trip and have face-to-face meetings with every design manager to get their personal commitment and buy-in to the schedule. He did this, and the project turned around. After meeting face-to-face and establishing a relationship and clear delegation (who had the monkey), the design managers started making their submittals. The construction design manager then held regular status meetings with the design managers to feed the monkeys and ensure the design submittals would be made on time.

HOW TO RECRUIT GOOD PEOPLE

You now know the positions you need and how you want people to perform, so the next questions are these: How do you recruit the right people? How can you see into their souls to know if they will perform with diligence, perseverance, and integrity?

As you build your team, you need to consider aptitude and attitude. In my industry, we've said for years that we would choose attitude (character, ability to work with others, no a-holes) over aptitude (technical skill) any day. Attitude is more important for lasting hires. Proverbs 27:17 states, "Iron sharpens iron, and one man sharpens another." You want team members who will make you a better project manager. You want to avoid hiring the wrong person who will cause your team more damage than good. Proverbs 26:10 says, "Like an archer who wounds everyone is one who hires a passing fool or drunkard." I'm sure we can all recall past bad hires and the pain they caused. So, don't be a bad archer and hire a passing fool who will wound your whole team. As a rule, you should be slow to hire and quick to fire.

I believe you can get both aptitude and attitude with the right process and questions. In a standard interview, you review a candidate's resume and experience and discuss what they learned and liked at each previous position and why they left. But that doesn't always get to who the person is.

Over the years, I have collected good questions to ask in an interview that help reveal a person's character, motives, dreams, and personality. Here are some of them:

- What specifically did you do to prepare for today's interview?
- What do you know about our company, our brand, leadership, history, future?
- How did you come to be who you are today?
- If you could only accomplish three measurable things before you die, what three things would they be?
- What's not on your resume that I should know about?
- What top three things annoy you about coworkers?
- Do you have any questions for me?[3]

Even after a fabulous interview with good answers to in-depth questions, you may still not have the right discernment to make the hire. Include other managers in the interview process so you can get input from those who have different insights than you. Because we had only a 50 percent success rate in recruiting and retaining entry-level engineers, my previous company completely changed the hiring process. We would only hire entry-level engineers after they interned with us for twelve weeks. To choose those interns, we did speed interviewing—twenty potential interns met with six different managers and five-year engineers for fifteen-minute interviews. We then collectively ranked them and made offers to ten of the twenty. The interns then came and worked on our jobsites with a mentor assigned to them. The interns needed time to evaluate construction as a career path, and we needed to observe them to see if they could make decisions and move forward in a chaotic environment. We then ended up offering full-time entry-level positions to approximately six interns.

If you don't have time to interview and hire properly, then don't do it. You will just create problems for yourself. I made this mistake when our team was desperate to hire a claims manager to pursue recovery of lost revenue. A member of my joint venture board provided a candidate. I interviewed him and decided he wasn't the right fit, but my executive insisted, "We have no other candidates. He's better than nobody." So, we hired him, but he ended up not being "better than nobody." He cost us a lot of time and wasted opportunities to recover revenue until we finally removed him from the project a year later.

Hire the best people you can. One of my first bosses said that he only hired the "best and brightest." I did strategic planning for a heavy civil contractor whose tagline was, "Be the Best—Build the Best." In long-term business, you can't split performance from character. You can always improve your performance, but it is very difficult to redeem character. Proverbs 9:8–9 states, "Do not reprove a scoffer, or he will hate you; reprove a wise man, and he will love you. Give instruction to a wise man, and he will be still wiser; teach a righteous man, and he will increase in learning." You must recruit people who are teachable. You want on your team those who are humble, hungry, and smart.[4] I firmly believe that these individuals exist, and you must not settle for less. Be slow to hire. Recruit those smarter and wiser than you who round out the team with different skill sets.

> **YOU MUST RECRUIT PEOPLE WHO ARE TEACHABLE.**

HOW TO HELP YOUR TEAM MAKE GOOD DECISIONS AND SOLVE PROBLEMS

How do you make good project decisions as a team and solve problems? Statistically, one would think that your decisions would be right at least 50 percent of the time—like flipping a coin and calling heads or tails. I have found that with the wrong dynamic in leadership, you can be wrong 70 percent of the time. If you view yourself as the smartest person in the room, you will make the wrong decision the vast majority of the time. Proverbs 18:1 states, "Whoever isolates himself seeks his own desire; he breaks out against all sound judgment." You desperately need input from sources other than yourself to make good, sound decisions on your project.

I worked with an insecure project manager who viewed himself as the smartest person on the project. When the engineers who were planning and performing the work gave him feedback on the path forward, he rejected their input because it was different from his own view of how to build the job. After a while, other managers stopped providing key feedback and input because it was never received well. As a result, critical decisions on the project often ended up costing more and taking longer than they should have. "Whoever trusts in his own mind is a fool, but he who walks in wisdom will be delivered" (Proverbs 28:26). If you want to forge a good path forward on your projects, do not trust in your own mind alone; be open to others' viewpoints.

How do you develop a culture and atmosphere of true collaboration and open brainstorming? The culture starts at the top of the organization. You must go into meetings to discuss problems with open-ended questions to solicit feedback. You need to model an open discussion by not shutting down others when they disagree with you. Many executives have very dominant personalities and can squash any discussion. I have dealt with executives in bid reviews of complex projects who dictated their opinions on cost and scope that had nothing to do with the project we were bidding. They just assumed it was similar to past projects. As an executive and a project manager, stay open to the ideas of others and listen and learn. After the decision is made, you can shut down dissenting viewpoints and discussion.

What happens to project managers and executives who bully their way on a project? They end up in failure because you can't make one bad decision after another and survive financially. Proverbs 11:2 states, "When pride comes, then comes disgrace, but with the humble is wisdom." If you are too proud to accept an opinion different from your own, you will be disgraced and removed from projects. Stay humble and realize that there are those with different viewpoints and experiences who can help you make good decisions.

Don't limit yourself by discouraging feedback. Intentionally develop and pursue key allies on your team who think differently than you. Nurture those who challenge you with a contrary perspective. They can both save your butt and help carry the emotional load of project management. It can be lonely operating alone; we must invest in allies. Proverbs 12:25 states, "Anxiety in a man's heart weighs him down, but a good word makes him glad." Your team can bring you a good word and carry the responsibility of completing the project. On large, complex projects, there is too much for one person to handle. I have tag-teamed with other managers who were just as strong as I. When one of us would get discouraged, the others would give a good word, and we would keep fighting to limit scope growth, change out personnel, and complete the project. This tag-team approach made the project bearable during difficult times.

> **IF YOU WANT TO FORGE A GOOD PATH FORWARD ON YOUR PROJECTS, DO NOT TRUST IN YOUR OWN MIND ALONE; BE OPEN TO OTHERS' VIEWPOINTS.**

Earlier in this chapter, I shared the story of how I made a wrong hire for a claims manager based on pressure from my joint venture board. When I finally removed this manager from the project, I found a superstar to take his place who turned the project around. How did this happen? Another joint venture executive asked me what his company could do to help. This executive was very strong, detailed, technically proficient, and frankly, better than I at claims. I asked him to come to the project and work full time to develop our large claim. I had to be okay with not being the guy on the large claim and let him be the expert and receive all the glory. This was my best decision on the project—getting someone stronger than I was to carry the load so I could focus on completing the project. Don't be afraid of hiring great people, resourcing them, and letting them shine.

CELEBRATE AND ENCOURAGE

Project management is fun! Make your project a great place to work by celebrating victories and encouraging your team through the tough periods on the project. People in general need encouragement and validation. So, as a project manager, how do you lead, encourage, and empower your team? Realize that all team member victories are project victories that should be celebrated.

> PEOPLE IN GENERAL NEED ENCOURAGEMENT AND VALIDATION.

Don't view praise and rewards from a mentality of scarcity thinking, *If I give her a reward for doing well, there is less remaining for myself.* Proverbs 3:27 states, "Do not withhold good from those to whom it is due, when it is in your power to do it." Plan short-term and long-term incentives for your key team members. Inform them of the bonus program for the company and for the project. Give them regular reviews and check in on how they are accomplishing their goals to keep them on track for their performance, then reward them accordingly.

Proverbs 25:13 states, "Like the cold of snow in the time of harvest is a faithful messenger to those who send him; he refreshes the soul of his masters." You cannot survive on your project without faithful managers who will take the initiative and follow through on what they said they would do. I tell my adult children that they will be stars at work if they do two things: (1) show up on time, and (2) do what they say they will do. Reward and praise your managers, and you will have faithful workers who want to work for the success of the project.

You should not only reward your managers but also celebrate with the workers. When we were close to opening the billion-dollar cable-stayed bridge, I knew politicians and executives would show up and take the credit for completing the project. I wanted to celebrate with the 250 craft who had worked so many long hours to build the bridge. I organized a lunch on the bridge during work hours with all the craft and my construction managers to celebrate their work and accomplishments. This celebration was one for the team and was much more meaningful than the opening celebration with the politicians.

When you celebrate with your team, you are doing more than just acknowledging their work. You are building a culture of recognition and gratitude. You are making your project the desired project to work on within your company. Whenever you give praise and rewards, they ironically circle back to you. When an executive tries to credit me for a job well done, I always defer and say it was a team victory and praise the people on the project who made it a success. This isn't false humility. I am truly thankful for the contributions of highly talented workers to my project.

CONCLUSION

The project manager is the leader of the team and sets the culture and vision for executing the project. The project is not about you but about recruiting, leading, and inspiring your team. You need an organizational chart with proper reporting of key discipline managers on your project. You must then properly delegate tasks and not be the source of all answers and direction on your project. Having been on projects with capable and poor personnel, you know how important it is to recruit

> # THE PROJECT IS NOT ABOUT YOU BUT ABOUT RECRUITING, LEADING, AND INSPIRING YOUR TEAM.

the right people who are a good long-term fit for your project and company. Now, go have fun being a project manager, creating something that did not exist before. Celebrate with your team as you make good decisions together and accomplish something you could never do on your own.

KEY ACTION ITEMS

1. **Define Your Organizational Chart and Direct Reports**—Determine the size of your team by evaluating how many people it takes to complete your project in the time allotted. Divide up the work based on the anticipated burn rate and technical discipline leads in your industry. Then determine your direct reports (no more than five) based on the critical path or greatest risk to manage the project successfully.

2. **Delegate Properly**—Give your direct reports the authority and responsibility to complete their tasks. Hold them accountable for their action items. Make sure they leave meetings with the monkey on their back and that you don't take on their tasks.

3. **Recruit the Right People**—Be quick to fire and slow to hire. Put time into recruiting and hiring the right people with a defined process of interviews and questions that get at the core of who people are and how they will perform under stress.

4. **Make Good Decisions**—Do not strive to be the smartest person in the room. Model open discussion until you can arrive at the right path forward with input from your team. Ask good questions to solicit honest feedback. Most of your managers don't have the confidence to tell you when you are wrong.

5. **Celebrate and Encourage**—Make your project the most desired project to work on by celebrating your team's victories. Plan these

celebrations to build team relationships and reward those who are excelling. Put together a short-term and long-term incentive plan and communicate it. Say "Thank you" and "Good job!" Positive acknowledgment often leads to higher employee satisfaction than more remuneration.

CHAPTER 4

PROTECT YOUR SCOPE AND MARGIN

"Whoever is simple, let him turn in here!" To him who lacks sense she says . . . "Leave your simple ways, and live, and walk in the way of insight."

PROVERBS 9:4–6

I vividly remember the first time a client started adding scope to my project. I was meeting with the client's representatives, who were older and more experienced than I. They had provided dozens of comments on the design, and we were reviewing our responses to their comments in the owner's office. The client's four seasoned managers instructed me and my lead designer to make changes that would cost millions of dollars more in construction. They asked us to design and build additional work because they said the contract required it. I assumed they were correct until I carefully read the contract and the specifications they referenced as justification for increasing the scope. The justification wasn't there! I then had an epiphany that has stuck with me for the rest of my life. These older and smarter engineers were simply stating their preferential opinions and wanted extra work for no additional cost. On top of that, the client paid them hourly to increase my scope, so they had no downside to asking me for more and holding back key approvals of the project to get what they wanted.

When you start your project, you're optimistic that you can complete the job with the budget and schedule assigned to you and turn a profit. You assemble the right team through hard work and effective recruitment. You create a working organizational chart with the correct number of direct reports. You then kick off the project, cast the vision, and establish a culture of working together and solving problems.

But problems start piling up against the project. You are prepared to deal with internal staff and technical problems, but you're not prepared to deal with external problems created by your client and the standard level of chaos that comes with new projects. Every project has external obstacles to overcome, whether from a change in field conditions, modifications to the performance criteria, schedule delays, or just pesky inspectors. There will always be issues that cost your project more time and money. It is naïve to be unprepared to deal with those who want to increase your scope for no additional cost and time. It is human nature for others to want you to work for free.

So, how do you plan to manage conflict and protect your scope while building the project?

In this chapter, we will discuss the need to be realistic about possible problems, scope creep, and delays. We will examine how to provide timely notice of potential issues and change orders while staying in relationship with your client. Then we will address how to prepare for conflict and adversity by building the right level of staffing to manage changes while you execute the project. Finally, we will discuss how to craft a strategy to win.

ANTICIPATE SCOPE CREEP AND DELAYS

It is simpleminded to think your project won't have scope growth that causes increased costs and schedule delays. Look again at the proverb opening this chapter: "'Whoever is simple, let him turn in here!' To him who lacks sense she says . . . 'Leave your simple ways, and live, and walk in the way of insight'" (Proverbs 9:4–6). This is a call to leave one's simple ways and walk in the way of wisdom. Being wise means anticipating that your project will face external problems, some quite complex. They shouldn't surprise you. If your project were easy, the client wouldn't need you.

> **IT IS SIMPLEMINDED TO THINK YOUR PROJECT WON'T HAVE SCOPE GROWTH THAT CAUSES INCREASED COSTS AND SCHEDULE DELAYS.**

As project managers, we are often optimistic about our relationship with our client, and we imagine we will be able to work out all change orders and schedule impacts at the end of the project. We assume the client will be fair since we've been fair with them. This, too, is a simple way of thinking, particularly since the client's representatives we work with and trust often leave the project before it is completed. It is important to document problems as they occur, accurately track costs, and put the client on notice of cost and schedule impacts. Without this documentation, you have no way of knowing the settlement amount for the change orders when the project is completed. If the project were based purely on a relationship and a handshake, then there would be no need for contracts, specifications, plans, and defined scopes of work.

As project manager, you need to be emotionally and organizationally prepared to provide notices of potential increases in costs due to an increase in the scope of work. My father was a contractor and loved to do favors for people. I worked with him building houses, and many times the owner of the house would want expensive fixtures in the bathrooms and kitchen. Of course, we didn't bid the job that way, and we had to tell the angry owners that these fixtures were not in the budget. My father, however, was never prepared for these conversations and often pleased the owners at his own expense. My mother would say that my father would get his crown in heaven because he certainly wasn't getting it here (based on what little profit he made). It would have been better for my father to have set a budget for fixtures at the time of the contract and let the owners decide how they wanted to spend the money. Or, if that hadn't been done, inform the owners as early as possible that the increase in scope would increase their costs.

Providing written notice of a potential change to the project notifies the client that they are causing problems and may be adding work that was not included in the original contract. The notice officially alerts both you and the client that costs and delays could be incurred and should be tracked. But it doesn't mean these problems *must* occur. The client could retract the comment or direction that is causing the issue.

I know many contractors in private commercial work abhor giving notice of potential changes because they worked hard to build the relationship that got them the invitation to bid the work. They are concerned that if they give notice, they won't be invited back to bid other projects. But you still need to have conversations, sometimes in writing, about scope growth. To minimize disruptions to the project and keep your client happy, state that your goal is to have no change orders so you can complete the project on schedule. Offer to prepare change orders only as a favor to your client. Then when you start the conversation about changes, you can remind the client that he requested it. This allows you to stay in relationship, which we will be focusing on in the next chapter.

On every project, you need to anticipate scope growth and project delays. Know that they are just part of life and prepare emotionally and organizationally to address them in a professional manner that preserves your relationships and allows you to continue to make progress on the project.

PROVIDE TIMELY NOTICE

As project manager, it is important for you to know when your contract requires you to give notice of potential changes. Many public works contracts require the contractor to provide written notice of a potential change within days of the discovery of the issue or, as stated in all capital letters:

> CONTRACTOR HEREBY EXPRESSLY WAIVES ALL RIGHTS TO ASSERT ANY AND ALL CLAIMS BASED ON ANY CHANGE IN THE WORK, DELAY, SUSPENSION, OR ACCELERATION . . . FOR WHICH CONTRACTOR FAILED TO PROVIDE PROPER AND TIMELY NOTICE AND AGREES THAT IT SHALL BE ENTITLED TO **NO COMPENSATION OR DAMAGES OR TIME EXTENSION WHATSO-EVER** IN CONNECTION WITH THE WORK.

Given these harsh contractual terms, the owners and clients should not be surprised when you provide notice of a potential change. They require it in the contract. But you may still hesitate to submit notices of potential changes for fear of damaging your work relationship with the client. The owner, however, has already established the terms of the relationship in the contractual language and placed in writing their expectation of proper contractual behavior.

You don't need to wait until you have all your ducks in a row to write a letter notifying the owner of a potential increase in costs. You just need to give notice so the client has the opportunity to mitigate the potential increase in costs and schedule by rescinding a comment or direction that is linked to the increase. When the owner's representative asks you why you are submitting notices of potential changes, just tell them you are following the contract and abiding by the terms they specified. If you missed the window to provide notice of a potential change or didn't clearly understand the client's direction, submit a Request for Information (RFI) to the owner. If the owner's answer

> **YOU DON'T NEED TO WAIT UNTIL YOU HAVE ALL YOUR DUCKS IN A ROW TO WRITE A LETTER NOTIFYING THE OWNER OF A POTENTIAL INCREASE IN COSTS.**

to the RFI confirms their direction, use their answer as the cause for sending timely notice.

As seasoned professionals, we often think we should have our whole story and argument of merit developed before we give our client notice of a potential change. This is a fallacy. We will never have our whole argument developed until we go before a third party to resolve issues that could not be resolved at the project level. The contract also doesn't allow you the necessary time to develop full-fledged arguments. You just need to give notice according to the contractual requirements.

On one project, two of the owner's representatives cornered me and asked why I was submitting so many notices of potential changes. I knew the notices were making them look bad because the claims were a direct result of their preferential comments during the design period that increased the scope and schedule. I told them, in full confidence, that the kindest thing I could do for them was to submit these timely notices. They gave me a mystified look, and I explained that I was providing them the opportunity to mitigate the costs, schedule, and impacts. That the notice of potential changes informed them *we* had a potential issue with costs and schedule. We didn't know yet who was responsible for this issue, but together we could work to mitigate, if not eliminate, the costs. I don't know if they ever believed that providing change notices was an act of kindness, but I was being proactive, protecting my client from uninformed exposure to risk created by their representatives.

To be able to provide timely notice, you need to have the proper level of staffing. Assign a contracts manager to write all notice letters to the client and keep records of correspondence for each issue and change notice. This doesn't mean that the contracts manager must know all the issues, just that they are responsible for getting notices out the door. In addition, don't feel you have to review all notice letters. Grant your contracts manager signature authority. This doesn't mean they can make commitments for you on costs, just on providing change notices to your clients. I can't tell you how satisfying it is to review correspondence and see change notices have been sent without my having to be involved.

"Where there is no guidance, a people falls, but in an abundance of counselors there is safety" (Proverbs 11:14). Use the varied expertise of your team to discern scope creep and deterioration of margin. The discipline managers that we discussed in Chapter 3 know their scope, specifications, plans, and design criteria better than you and your contracts manager. They are your counselors who should protect you. Give your discipline managers the authority to issue unofficial email notices of potential changes to their counterparts on the project. These email notices can subsequently be turned into official notices of change. You need your whole team's participation not only to execute the project but also to protect the scope and margin of your project.

Proverbs 15:2 states, "The tongue of the wise commends knowledge, but the mouths of fools pour out folly." Be prepared to state the reasons for your change notice and don't just shoot from the hip. Be thoughtful in what you say, or your client may begin to lose faith in your abilities and credibility; however, you have the contractual right to be wrong. I have told the owner's representatives multiple times, "We might be wrong, but we are now tracking costs and time in the event that this issue becomes a claim." This statement helps keep me in good standing with my client. If your work is negotiated and based on invitations to bid, you must tread carefully and state that per your subcontracts, you have the obligation to pass on your subcontractor's claims, but you will do everything you can to minimize the costs and impacts.

Finally, do not destroy your relationship with your client by sending letter after letter of change notices. Let your client know before you throw a grenade over the wall in the form of a change notice. This is a key value of partnering on projects. Pick up the phone and call your client to tell them a letter is coming. This will help preserve your relationship. The client needs to know you are operating in good faith and not manipulating the contract to get more money.

I had to make one of those unpleasant calls to inform my client I was suing them. The client was not complying with the provisions for addressing disputes during the project. They were in breach of the contract, and we had no way of moving forward to resolve issues. It's unusual—and extremely challenging—to sue a client while a project is ongoing, but I made the call and told the client we were suing them at the direction of my joint venture executives. I reiterated that I was committed to completing the project and couldn't complete it without his help. He said he understood and that he, too, needed my help to complete the project. This call helped launch us on the trajectory to complete the project and resolve our issues at the project level.

PREPARE FOR CONFLICT

Sadly, today's business and construction environment of overregulation and scarcity of resources makes conflict inevitable. Don't be surprised to find yourself spending 60 percent of your time dealing with both internal and external conflicts. Usually, you can manage internal conflict because you have built up deposits of trust with your company and

> **YOU WILL FAIL AT MANAGING EXTERNAL CONFLICTS IF YOU DO NOT PREPARE FOR THEM.**

executives to weather tough projects. But you will fail at managing external conflicts if you do not prepare for them. As I stated in the opening chapter, one of my difficult projects depleted my health and put me in the hospital because I wasn't ready to manage the conflict. I didn't have the processes or staff in place to be successful.

"The wisdom of the prudent is to discern his way, but the folly of fools is deceiving" (Proverbs 14:8). Being prudent is considering your path and planning for a successful project.

Build Your Change Management Team—Consider the organization and level of staffing you need to process change orders. Usually, executives of organizations do not consider this commitment of staff until cash flow issues develop and the project starts making cash calls because it cannot pay its bills.

I have a friend who only does commercial construction, and he despises change orders because they cost money and time for his staff to put together. This same staff manages all the subcontractors doing the work, so he sees preparing change orders as a distraction. My friend's shortcoming is that he does not staff his projects to address owner-requested change orders.

So plan ahead and get the staff in place. You already have a contracts manager taking care of correspondence. This person can offer some help preparing change orders and merit arguments, but you need a dedicated staff.

After giving timely notice (as discussed above), the next step required is a repository of correspondence organized by issue or change notice. You don't have time to look for documents and store them yourself. Assign an administrative assistant who works for your contracts manager to create electronic issue folders. Set up folders and organize them by correspondence date. Then combine them into a single bookmarked document. This allows you to quickly read or scan six months of correspondence and get up to speed on the issue and decide the next steps to take.

Appoint a claims or engineering manager or a deputy project manager to manage your claims team. Then add an estimator, cost engineer, and schedule engineer who can price change orders and prepare time impact analyses. You can add consultants and construction attorneys to supplement your staff, but I don't suggest you start with them. If the conflicts involve millions of dollars, then you will need consultants and lawyers to help prosecute your claims. Be careful whom you bring on your team for change management. Sometimes your executives won't want to spend the money it takes to place the right level of talented personnel on claims recovery. Proverbs 10:26 states, "Like vinegar to the teeth and smoke to the eyes, so is the sluggard to those who send him." I have had these types of people on my projects, and they are very painful to deal with.

What type of individual do you want to lead the claims team? You want a leader who spends time doing forensic work slogging through the muck of losses and crafting a story of disruption and delay. This unique individual must be willing to perform tedious work but also understand how projects are supposed to operate. They must be discerning and meticulous, sniffing out the slow, insipid scope creep and documenting how it occurred. This leader must be willing to put their head down and work. On one claims intensive job, my deputy project manager had all these talents and skills and worked tirelessly to bring definition to our changes. He joked that he was like "Mater" the tow truck in the animated movie *Cars* who was always backing up to attach a winch to broken-down cars. Like Mater, he was constantly driving backward, gathering past cost and schedule damages caused by the owner's directions and interference. Managing claims is not glorious work, but it is essential for large, complex projects. I will be forever grateful for having a Mater as part of my team.

Don't Antagonize Your Client—"A brother offended is more unyielding than a strong city, and quarreling is like the bars of a castle" (Proverbs 18:19). Always stay professional and courteous in your written and spoken communications with your client. If you feel the need to write a strong letter, do so, but don't send it for a few days. I suggest having your spouse or a friend unaffiliated with your project read the letter to obtain an unbiased and, hopefully, more emotionally balanced viewpoint. Don't intentionally offend your clients (or executives) because

> ALWAYS STAY PROFESSIONAL AND COURTEOUS IN YOUR WRITTEN AND SPOKEN COMMUNICATIONS WITH YOUR CLIENT.

"They deserve it!" based on their behavior. Don't get polarized and quietly refer to your client as an idiot or an a-hole. You won't be able to hide your disdain for them, and you may end up being removed from the project. If you screw up and say something in anger, apologize. But realize once something comes out of your mouth, it can't be taken back.

I had a colleague who didn't respect the owner's representatives and referred to them as worthless. He had spent time in the South where he picked up a saying: "They ain't worth killing." In other words, some critters aren't worth wasting a bullet on. In one contentious meeting, my colleague told the owner that his inspectors "ain't worth killing." Needless to say, that wasn't well received.

When you must talk to the client about the potential change orders and scope growth they are causing, remind them of the overall goals of the project—completing the project on time and on budget. Discuss progress and ways to re-sequence your work and mitigate delays and costs. Ask them to help relax some of the criteria (without compromising quality or reducing the scope) that will accelerate the work. Make your client a partner in completing the project.

> ## MAKE YOUR CLIENT A PARTNER IN COMPLETING THE PROJECT.

"Whoever meddles in a quarrel not his own is like one who takes a passing dog by the ears" (Proverbs 26:17). Strive to keep the conflicts with the client or internal executives limited to completing the project. Stay on point for your claims. Don't fight others' battles. There may be issues on your project with the client's other stakeholders or internal politics with executives. Leave these issues alone and don't get drawn into them. They are a complete waste of time and needlessly expend your goodwill capital that should only be used for the project's issues.

I knew a bright project manager who excelled at claims, but he took everything as a personal affront to his intelligence. He was not only determined to win, but he wanted to let the client's representatives know he was winning. So he needlessly picked fights with them and agitated them until they no longer wanted to deal with him. No matter how well positioned you are at establishing the merit and costs for owner-caused changes, you always need good will from the owner to finalize and issue change orders. Therefore, do not antagonize your client!

Avoid Overreactions—Finding the right path to manage potential changes to the job is difficult. We are prone to overreact—to either claim everything or claim nothing. Remember the story of *Goldilocks and the Three Bears*? Goldilocks came upon a cabin in the woods and sampled three bowls of porridge—one was too hot, one was too cold, and the third was just right. She sat in three chairs and tried three beds—Papa Bear's was too hard, Mama Bear's was too soft, and Baby Bear's was just right (so she lay down in Baby Bear's bed and took a nap). You want to be "just right" in your claims management.

Too Hard—Don't be like Papa Bear's bed and be "too hard" by claiming everything in sight. I know an extremely aggressive contractor who starts the job with a staff of five lawyers ready to fight on every issue from day one. Life is too short to make everything a conflict and always be in a fight. This contractor has a bad reputation in the industry, and very few other contractors want to partner with him on large projects. If you make a claim out of everything, there is no distinction between fake issues and real issues.

Too Soft—Don't be like Mama Bear's bed and be "too soft," claiming nothing on your projects in an attempt to stay in good relationship with your client. And don't assume your client has the same values and authority to make these contractual decisions as you do. Many high-level project managers are honorable people who want to do the right thing. They want to partner with their client and base any changes on a handshake and their word, but that is naïve and unwise.

I worked on a complex job with a very honorable project manager who set up executive partnering with the client to resolve issues. He assumed the client was just as honorable. As part of the executive partnering guidelines, lawyers were not to be involved in the meetings, and everything discussed was to remain confidential and not be used in any future arbitration. When we were negotiating claims at the end of the project, however, we learned that the client's executives were taking confidential issues discussed in the meetings to their legal team for advice, and the lawyers had sabotaged the process by strongly advising they deny everything.

Don't be too soft! You must document issues to reserve your rights and have a record to establish merit when you settle at the end of the project. You can still conduct executive partnering to stay in relationship and establish goodwill to resolve issues, but write simple letters to establish a written record to protect yourself.

Just Right—Strive to have the Goldilocks approach in managing changes: "just right." Don't make claims out of everything. Provide your client the opportunity to reduce costs by informing them of potential issues with change notices. You will have to decide what is "just right" for your project, client, and company. But realize we are all human and prone to overreaction because we are emotionally vested in our projects. Be just right!

STRATEGIZE HOW TO WIN

Your goal is to win your claims for change orders, but you need to develop a strategy and know your own limitations. "The one who states his case first seems right, until the other comes and examines him" (Proverbs 18:17). We start off firmly believing our read of the contract is correct and that there could be no other reasonable interpretation. But as my favorite contractual mentor always said, "Never fall in love with your own argument!" We can easily deceive ourselves. Most likely, your argument to justify a change order has holes in it, but you may not see them because you lack perspective and have convinced yourself that your reasoning is sound. So, what are you to do when you are confident your con-

> **NEVER FALL IN LOVE WITH YOUR OWN ARGUMENT!**

tractual interpretations are absolutely correct? Get input from other senior managers or construction lawyers.

You will only receive feedback if you ask for it or if your executives are tracking the risks in recovering lost dollars and time. I have had good help and poor help developing strategies for the recovery of large claims. You are responsible for getting good help. Don't just go through the motions of having someone review your strategy and merit arguments. The best help is to find someone smarter than you to take an independent read on the contract, design criteria, and specifications, then examine the arguments.

You may need to hire construction lawyers for the prosecution of your claim. Your issues may not be solved at the project level but end up in arbitration or court. If your claim goes to arbitration, this changes the rules of discovery and your use of experts. You may need to assign your merit and quantum experts as exclusive consultants to your legal team for the development of your claim.

On one project, it took me over eighteen months to find the right construction lawyer with the skill set and temperament to dive into the issues to determine the strengths and weaknesses of our position. Based on his analysis and input from independent experts, we developed a strategy that focused on the strengths of our claim and minimized our weaknesses by staying silent on those issues. Our strategy was to let the client mention these issues and then rebut them if necessary. We thought we had a clear understanding of our risk of losing the claim. It wasn't until after we reached a global settlement with the client that we realized we had significant exposure due to some of our own team members' actions.

Lawyers are needed for counsel on large complex claims. But because they are so risk averse, they often struggle to make timely decisions. Never turn over the leadership of your change order process to lawyers. You should always be out front leading, with the legal team behind you. A primary skill set you have as a project manager is the ability to identify, price, and manage risk. Never defer this leadership to lawyers.

In developing your strategy, realize that you live or die by the contract, and you can never go wrong by following the contract; therefore, always lead from the position that you are implementing the contract your client wrote. Be cautious not to fall into the trap that the contract is ambiguous, or you may lose your argument in court. Since you are an expert in your field of work, it is problematic to argue ambiguity—that you didn't understand the scope of work for which you are an expert. If you lose your argument, you won't be able to recover direct and indirect costs for schedule delays. In the midst of determining the merit of a claim on one of my difficult projects, the owner asked me if I thought the specification was ambiguous. Since I had spent time strategizing how to recover the large claim due to this poorly written specification, I told him, "No, we understand the contract and followed it." Our strategy paid off, and we were able to prevail and reach a fair settlement.

CONCLUSION

This chapter was painful for me to write. It brought up bad memories of projects I worked on where protection of scope and recovery of margin were poorly executed. As you grow in your career, you will spend more and more time mitigating losses and strategizing how to recover costs from your client.

This chapter might have also offended you. You may think it is dishonorable to grasp for profit through change orders. But realize, as the project manager, you have the fiduciary responsibility to your company to not give away the margin of the project and incur risk of losses. In managing the scope of work, you are not being greedy; rather, you are acting within the trust granted to you by your executives.

Early in my career, I worried about appearing political and working owners and projects for my own career growth. I developed my personal integrity test to get clarity on my actions. I would ask myself, *Am I fighting for this change order for my glory or to meet the fiduciary obligations of my position?* Knowing that my actions were not for my own financial benefit but for the good of the project empowered me to fight for a fair outcome more easily and thoroughly.

Most of us pursued project management because of our skill sets and because it was fun. But to serve the rest of your team and build the project, you must plan for conflict so it doesn't distract you from completing your project and earning your margin/profit. Always be truthful in your representation of claims and do nothing that is false.

KEY ACTION ITEMS

1. **Anticipate Scope Creep and Delays**—If you are managing a project, the client or their representatives will want you to add scope and do it for free. Don't be surprised at this request. Expect it and plan for it. Be emotionally and organizationally prepared to provide a written notice of a potential increase in costs due to an increase in the scope of work.

2. **Provide Timely Notice**—Assign a manager to be responsible for making all written notices required by your contract. Use the vast experience of your team and discipline managers to email the claims manager on notices that need to be sent out. Authorize your field leads to email notice of changes in field conditions to the owner's representatives. Remember that you are being kind to provide timely notice in compliance with the contract to allow your client to reduce cost and schedule impacts.

3. **Prepare for Conflict**—Prepare your project management organization (estimator, scheduler, cost engineer) to deal with change orders and recovery. Assign an administrative assistant under your contracts manager to prepare a bookmarked document of all correspondence (organized by date). Do not antagonize your client in your correspondence and communications. Stay professional and

courteous. Bring your client into the strategy of mitigating delays and completing the project on time.

4. **Strategize to Win**—Realize that you are not God's gift to change management. Get input and critiques from senior managers and lawyers (if necessary) on your merit argument. Assign senior key leaders or construction lawyers to prepare your claims. Plan for arbitration with the right level of protection for your key experts. Do not abdicate leadership. Stay involved and lead!

CHAPTER 5

RELATIONSHIPS ARE YOUR BIGGEST ASSET

He who loves purity of heart, and whose speech is gracious, will have the king as his friend.

PROVERBS 22:11

A man who is kind benefits himself, but a cruel man hurts himself.

PROVERBS 11:17

I have a colleague who always complains that his clients are slowing down work and not paying for changes and that his young engineers are lazy and don't want to work. Whenever I ask how he is doing, he rants about how people are screwing up his life. His philosophy is "All people suck."

What a miserable way to go through life when you have no choice but to interact with people every day.

I cannot overstate the importance of staying in good relationship with your team members and your client to manage a project well. Why? Because you can't build the project by yourself. You are dependent upon people. Sometimes you may be tempted to think that project management would be great if it weren't for the people. Yes, you will most likely have problems with your personnel and challenging relationships with your client, but I encourage you to cultivate a positive attitude with those relationships. In project management, you have the great privilege of working with incredibly talented, dysfunctional people. The sheer entertainment value is worth the price of admission. I have met one-of-a-kind managers, engineers, superintendents, and clients that don't fit any category of people I normally run into. So, enjoy the dysfunction, chaos, and process of creating something as a team that you could never achieve on your own.

> YOU HAVE THE GREAT PRIVILEGE OF WORKING WITH INCREDIBLY TALENTED, DYSFUNCTIONAL PEOPLE. THE SHEER ENTERTAINMENT VALUE IS WORTH THE PRICE OF ADMISSION.

Realize, too, that even if you were able to assemble the perfect team with the perfect client who will partner with you to complete the project ahead of schedule and below budget, the team would no longer be perfect once you joined it. We are not perfect! I have failed. You will fail, and you will need grace and mercy from your client and executives when you screw up. The only mitigation for your future failures is your relationships. Have you invested in them so that when your project goes sideways, your client will work with you to fix the problem? Proverbs 10:12 states, "Hatred stirs up strife, but love covers all offenses." Relationships cover a multitude of offenses.

In this chapter we will examine how to genuinely love people, which is the basis for all relationships. Next, we will look at practical steps to develop effective relationships on the job. Then we will discuss how to become a person of peace who is safe, approachable, winsome, and a confidant. These qualities will serve you well as you lead and build the project.

Life is too short not to enjoy the vast kaleidoscope of people you get to work with. I encourage you to invest in relationships that will benefit you for a lifetime.

GENUINELY LOVE PEOPLE

I know it sounds strange to say that you need to genuinely love people. But if you want authentic, lasting relationships with clients, colleagues, and executives, you need to demonstrate an attitude of wanting what is best for them. That's what love is—wanting what is best for the other person. You must actually care about the people you work with and demonstrate that you want success for those who sit across the table from you. To love somebody is to wish a blessed life for them.

You may have heard the love passage—1 Corinthians 13—read at a wedding, but it is worth reviewing here to be reminded of what love looks like. In his epistle to the Corinthians, the Apostle Paul wasn't writing about romantic love; he was putting flesh and bones on what Jesus taught about loving one another. So, as you read the following verses, do so in the context of difficult relationships with your client's representatives, employees, or irritating bosses: "Love is patient and kind; love does not envy or boast; it is not arrogant or rude. It does not insist on its own way; it is not irritable or resentful; it does not rejoice at wrongdoing but rejoices with the truth. Love bears all things, believes all things, hopes all things, endures all things" (1 Corinthians 13:4–7).

Notice how love is other-focused and not about how *I* should be treated. This may seem like a weak posture in an aggressive industry. But considering the welfare of others doesn't mean you compromise the project.

I have worked with representatives of the owner who needed to be removed from the job because they were obstructing the project and increasing the owner's risk. One engineer would make excessive, contractually argumentative comments in his review of the design. He was not operating within his authority and expertise, and he was causing great strife with the whole project. I didn't wish ill for him, but I wanted him to be corrected by the owner and stay in his technical review lane. I took the owner aside and reviewed this engineer's comments with him. I told the owner to rein him in because he was pouring gasoline on an issue and escalating a conflict with a key stakeholder. The owner did not take my advice, and several months later, the engineer was removed in disgrace because of the damage he had caused the project. My attempts at corrective action were out of love. If the engineer's behavior had been addressed earlier, he could have left the project with his reputation intact.

It is not wrong to decide that some people on your team and the client's team are too difficult to work with and should be moved to another project. To respectfully manage this conflict, always keep in mind what is best for the project, the person, and their career.

> **ALWAYS KEEP IN MIND WHAT IS BEST FOR THE PROJECT, THE PERSON, AND THEIR CAREER.**

If you want to have great influence in your organization and be the project manager of choice for your client, love people well as you build your project. Demonstrate that you care both for the project and for the people on the project. Your client needs to know that you are not an a-hole in your heart of hearts. Proverbs 22:11 reaffirms the value and influence of love: "He who loves purity of heart, and whose speech is gracious, will have the king as his friend."

Be Kind for the Sake of Being Kind—You may be concerned that you will appear weak if you choose to be kind to others. But it takes incredible strength and control to show kindness. When you choose to be kind, your kindness returns to you. Proverbs 11:17 states, "A man who is kind benefits himself, but a cruel man hurts himself." This echoes a popular saying—"What goes around, comes around," which means when you are cruel, people at some point will be cruel to you. Kindness ultimately benefits the project by creating allies who will help you complete the project.

If you are honest with yourself, you recognize that you would not be where you are today if it weren't for the kindness of others. Stop and think about a mentor, parent, teacher, or friend who showed you kindness. Were you deserving of this kindness, or was it a gift? I remember one of my early construction mentors who would not allow me to confuse revenue with costs. At the time, I was irritated with him. Later, however, I was thankful for his kindness of challenging me until I finally understood the difference between revenue and cost.

We have a choice in how we treat people. Sometimes we show kindness to those in power, and we hope for reciprocity—that they will in turn treat us well. But it is better to be kind to those below you in the organization. Many of us in a position of power choose to ignore those beneath us and treat them as servants or cogs in the wheel. Instead, demonstrate wisdom, knowing these same people may one day become your clients, and be kind to them because it is the right thing to do. Be kind for the sake of being kind.

One company I worked for preferred to staff administrative positions through temporary employment agencies. But these temporary agencies didn't pay for health care or vacations. Amy was a capable temp employee who processed all our design changes and requests for information. After working for me for several months, Amy had clearly proven her value to the project. I wanted to hire her as a full-time employee, but my company didn't want to take on that cost. She brought value to the job, but beyond that, she was a single mother of three who needed the benefits. Believing that hiring her was the right thing to do, I fought for months and had several contentious discussions with my boss until finally the company agreed. Amy ended up being a great asset to the project, proactively administering all the field and design changes and keeping the project on schedule.

I also choose to build good relationships with the gatekeepers of my client's calendar, often having a better relationship with them than they have with their boss. I work with these very capable administrative gatekeepers to set up meetings. These wonderful sources of information tell me how my client is doing before I talk to them, which helps me have productive conversations and not antagonize my client on a bad day.

Be kind by doing good to others.

Empathize with Your Client and Team—In project management and construction, empathy for others is often lacking. We tend to treat people as tools whose purpose is to accomplish our daily and overall goals: they are useful, or we discard them. Empathy is "the action of understanding, being aware of, being sensitive to, and vicariously experiencing the feelings, thoughts, and experience of another."[5] I encourage you to see your team members and clients as people with a myriad of other struggles in their professional and personal lives. They don't just exist to administer and construct your project.

On one of my large, complex projects, I noticed that the executive from the Department of Transportation had missed the last quarterly partnering session and was unusually distracted at our next meeting. During a session break, I asked her how she was doing, assuming her past absence was due to professional reasons; instead, she shared that she had taken four weeks off work because her husband had passed away. Her grief was noticeably deep and fresh, so I sought to encourage her. I told her she was fortunate to have a real loss to grieve, to have had such a great marriage and family, and I assured her I would pray for God to hold her through her grief. She started to weep in that hallway outside our meeting, and I thought, *What have I done?* But all I did was enter into her grief, empathize with her, and speak kind words that brought comfort to her during a difficult time.

Empathy is also critical with new hires and young engineers. We often expect them to be just like we were when we started out, but they are from different generations. I recently spoke with a college career counselor who said that the generation currently coming out of college is the most insecure and fearful she has ever seen. She said the students are afraid of being "canceled" for saying or doing something wrong. Because these graduates are afraid of today's cancel culture and haven't had real-world experience, they won't ask questions. By empathizing with our new hires and young engineers and mentoring them, we can help them grow in their confidence and competence.

BUILD EFFECTIVE RELATIONSHIPS

Many of us are not good at building relationships because we see them as a distraction to being productive in our jobs. We may have hundreds of contacts, but we don't make use of them. We meet people and move on to the next project. I encourage you to be intentional about building and maintaining relationships in your business.

Treat People How You Want to Be Treated—Remember the Golden Rule? "Whatever you wish that others would do to you, do also to them . . ." (Matthew 7:12). Our elementary school teachers drilled this principle into us to make us get along, and it does just that. I told my kids when they were growing up that to make new friends, they had to first be friends by treating others well. Part of building relationships is caring for and acting toward people the way you want to be treated.

You can do this while managing your projects. One reviewer I worked with was very difficult and considered himself more technically competent than anyone else. In meetings, I would agree with him on issues that I could, saying, "Sam is right, we will incorporate his comments." When he pushed for design improvements that were not part of the scope, I spoke with him in private to explain why I disagreed with him. I treated him how I wanted to be treated—with respect and without public embarrassment—and it preserved our professional relationship.

An inspector in the field once told me, "Let's admit it, Bob. I'm a bastard and so are you." I replied, "Oh, Dave, give me a hug." From this interaction, we learned how to work together even though we had disagreements.

Treating people well can be especially challenging when conveying bad news. When you must tell your client that something has gone wrong on the project, it is best to talk to them in person or on the phone. The worst action is to send them an email after business hours. Emails are too open to miscommunication and offense.

On my projects, I make a habit of visiting my client in person (not at a meeting) once a week just to check in. My actions show that I value the client enough to greet them in person and visit them on a regular basis, which establishes a relationship with them. Then when there is bad news, I call my client to let them know what went wrong so they have enough details to inform their executives. I always own the problem and tell them we are addressing the issue. I treat my clients how I want to be treated.

Create Long-Term Relationships—Remember those hundreds of contacts you have that I mentioned earlier? I recommend you view all your contacts with your colleagues, clients, and their representatives as long-term relationships in which both parties can benefit.

For those contacts to become friends, you need to intentionally nurture those relationships. The best way I have found to get outside of the work bubble and build friendships is to have a meal together. As humans, there is something about breaking bread together that forms deep connections. Sharing a meal reminds us of eating meals with our family growing up. It also acknowledges our collective need for sustenance. Sharing a meal is enjoyable, and it is difficult to be angry with someone when we are eating. Conversations naturally move beyond the project, and having our mouths filled with food helps us control what we say. There have been many occasions when I was glad I couldn't speak due to a mouthful of hamburger or steak, and someone else mercifully changed the direction of the conversation.

> THERE IS SOMETHING ABOUT BREAKING BREAD TOGETHER THAT FORMS DEEP CONNECTIONS.

The basis for all relationships is trust, which comes from spending time together. Meeting in a conference room can sometimes be too formal and restrictive to reach agreements. I have found that the most successful executive partnering often occurs over drinks and hors d'oeuvres after the official partnering sessions. We joke in construction that beer brings clarity. (But I suggest you don't have more than two beers, or you'll forget the clarity you just achieved.) Plan to go to lunch with your client's representatives, and don't just talk shop the whole time. Ask about their family, children, vacations, and life outside of work.

If you play any type of sport, it is great to do this with your team and client. Sports form deep connections and provide great insight into the character of a person. Is he an angry person? Does she get competitive and hate losing? Are they team players or just looking for their own glory? I played racquetball for years with Mike, the chief engineer of one of my clients, and Brian, his consultant representative. This helped forge a lasting relationship and good memories. I ran into Brian recently on a project I'm consulting on. He works on the owner's side, and because of our relationship, I was able to sit down and get an honest perspective from him on how the contractor (my client) was doing on the project. You can't put a monetary value on relationships. They always benefit you, whether in friendship or in business.

> YOU CAN'T PUT A MONETARY VALUE ON RELATIONSHIPS. THEY ALWAYS BENEFIT YOU, WHETHER IN FRIENDSHIP OR IN BUSINESS.

On one of my largest projects, we were able to develop a unique staging solution that mitigated nine months of delays because I had established a good and respectful relationship with my client. Per the contract, only one freeway connector could be demolished at a time until we opened the newly constructed connector. But we were delayed on the project due to another issue. I told my client that to make up time, we wanted to demolish the other connector and detour the traffic to a local arterial street. I asked for his help managing his engineering staff who were against the idea because it hadn't been done before. I told my engineering consultant to design the detour so conservatively that it would not give the client's engineers a technical reason to say no. We then constructed the detour and tested it with traffic before we took down the connector and started building the new viaduct. Because of mutual trust, my client and I were able to open the facility to the public earlier and mitigate the costs of delays. This could not have happened without having a good relationship with my client.

Build Proactive Relationships with Difficult Subs and Vendors— Some of your most difficult business relationships may be with problematic subcontractors and vendors who blame their problems and delays on you. Proverbs 19:11 states, "Good sense makes one slow to anger, and it is his glory to overlook an offense." At times you may be tempted to tell them to go screw themselves, but let wisdom prevail— and don't do it. You must stay in a good working relationship with your subs and vendors because, in the end, they can do more to hurt your project through delays than you can harm them. I am not saying to be weak and cave into their demands; rather, preserve the relationship so you can work through the difficult issues while making the right financial decisions for your project.

I had a steel provider on a technical bridge project who was behind schedule and could not meet the terms of the $55 million purchase order/subcontract. We even bonded them to help ensure their performance, but they were not up to the task. I could have terminated them for cause, but then I would have had to start over with another vendor, which would have caused another year of delay and the preparation of thousands of shop drawings. So, what was I to do? I kept a civil relationship so we could have difficult conversations and forge a path forward. I helped them with their cash flow by paying for their justified change orders before my client approved them to keep them financially afloat and assisted them with schedule relief where I could. Whenever their owner called and threatened me (with multiple f-bombs) to never send any steel again unless I paid him, I stayed calm and focused on solutions. I couldn't respond in kind because his performance was critical to the success of the job.

On the same project, I had a difficult rebar subcontractor who was to provide and install millions of pounds of rebar. He put together a $16 million claim against me and started a lawsuit. We ended up settling for $2 million due to reconciliation of quantities. During this extreme bad-faith behavior, I kept a professional relationship because I still needed him to execute his work on the project. I paid his invoices on time and worked with him to resolve technical issues that would cost him more money. At the end of day, he was willing to settle without going to court.

For our projects to succeed, we have no choice but to purposefully stay in relationship with difficult clients, subcontractors, and vendors. We must swallow our pride and do what is best to complete the project. We must be the adults in the relationship, which can be tiring. But it is very satisfying to work through hard relationships and prevail by completing the project. Choose to intentionally build relationships and be someone with whom people want to work and be friends.

> **FOR OUR PROJECTS TO SUCCEED, WE HAVE NO CHOICE BUT TO PURPOSEFULLY STAY IN RELATIONSHIP WITH DIFFICULT CLIENTS, SUBCONTRACTORS, AND VENDORS.**

BE A PERSON OF PEACE

In the ancient world, there were very few hotels or inns. When traveling, a sojourner would gather at the city gate and wait for someone to invite him to stay at their home. The traveler was looking for a person of peace who would be hospitable and offer shelter and protection. It was dangerous to stay outside overnight in the ancient world.

In the same way, to be a successful project manager, you want to be seen as a person of peace to whom others come for counsel, solutions, and hospitality. A person of peace is safe, approachable, winsome, and a confidant—someone whose counsel and wisdom are valued.

Be a Safe Person—"A man of wrath stirs up strife, and one given to anger causes much transgression" (Proverbs 29:22). You know people like this in your business and family, and you purposefully avoid them because they are not safe people. Another familiar but true proverb is "A fool's lips walk into a fight, and his mouth invites a beating" (Proverbs 18:6). Many of us have had friends or siblings like this who always started fights with their words. As a project manager, you don't want to be a person who is always starting skirmishes because you can't control what you say when you're angry.

You want to be one who is slow to anger. Proverbs 15:18 says, "A hot-tempered man stirs up strife, but he who is slow to anger quiets contention." Remaining calm when things get heated demonstrates your wisdom and understanding to those around you. You are seen as a strong leader and a safe person by not vomiting vitriol at the slightest insult.

As project manager of one of my largest jobs, I led project meetings with my client and his third-party representatives. These were difficult meetings because the representatives always wanted something for free or favors for their tenants adjacent to the project. In one meeting, an aggressive representative accused me of lying to him, stating that I had promised something in the previous meeting and never delivered. I became angry at his clearly false accusation. I felt my face turning red, tension in my neck, and vitriol working its way up my throat. I was ready to tell this guy what to do with certain body parts and where he should spend eternity. Instead, I ended the meeting, got up, and walked out. It was awkward walking out of my own meeting, but it was the best option to stay professional.

If you can't control angry words from coming out of your mouth, put yourself in time-out. My wife and I used time-outs with our young children to help them calm down and get control of their emotions. This also works for adults who have no emotional reserves left to deal with idiots. (I shouldn't have said idiots.) Remember, you always have the option to stay quiet and walk out of your own meeting.

Be a safe person, someone people are not afraid to be around. If you want your project to succeed, you cannot be an angry person who stirs up strife.

Be Approachable—In addition to being safe, you want to be seen as approachable. It's important that your client and those who work for you want to come talk to you rather than avoid you. That way, you will hear about problems early on and have open communication on how best to solve those problems. Being approachable is about more than being a safe person. It is an attitude of inviting conversation and solutions. It is not being threatened by those who have better ideas than you.

Being approachable is not just being pleasant to be with; it is saying the right thing at the right time. "A soft answer turns away wrath, but a harsh word stirs up anger" (Proverbs 15:1). We can either add gasoline to the fire or extinguish it by how we act and what we say. It is easy to be calm when we are not in the middle of a quarrel. Before conflict starts, develop phrases or responses you can use in an argument such as, "Thank you for that observation. Give me some time to

> **BEING APPROACHABLE IS ABOUT MORE THAN BEING A SAFE PERSON. IT IS AN ATTITUDE OF INVITING CONVERSATION AND SOLUTIONS.**

consider it, and I will get back to you." Or, "Interesting viewpoint. Let me check with my staff, and I will give you a call." Or my favorite humorous response: "My wife has said similar things to me. Let me check with her to confirm the validity of your criticism."

Keep your office door open for people to come and talk with you. On one of my largest jobs, I had a small round table in my office that was always clear of clutter. When the client came by to talk, I could get out from behind my desk and sit at that table with him. I always wanted to be approachable so we could solve issues one-on-one instead of in meetings.

Be Winsome—In addition to being safe and approachable, you want to be winsome. To be winsome is to be cheerful and lighthearted. Merriam-Webster Dictionary defines it as "generally pleasing and engaging."[6] To be winsome is to be likable—so much so that others want to be with you and help you. It is all about having a good attitude and being an optimist. Proverbs 16:24 states, "Gracious words are like a honeycomb, sweetness to the soul and health to the body." You can choose to be cheerful or cynical. You don't need to become a grumpy old man or woman before your time.

When you are winsome, people want to be with you and share their lives with you. They not only like your disposition, but they also respect your advice. Proverbs 12:18 says, "There is one whose rash words are like sword thrusts, but the tongue of the wise brings healing." If people like you, they will be motivated to work with you and perform good work. Being winsome opens doors with your clients and employees. It gains trust.

We had a cantankerous third-party safety representative, Tom, who didn't have a good relationship with anyone on the project except for Jimmy. Jimmy was winsome and patient, and Tom trusted Jimmy because he would listen and assure Tom of the many precautions being taken to make a very challenging job safe. Whenever any other managers had problems getting along with Tom (who liked to tell them what to do), we would send Jimmy in to calm things down.

When you are winsome, people want to work with you to help you succeed. At the end of a project, my client wanted me to clear a paved construction yard of 300,000 cubic yards of spoils to make space for storage containers. We had no place to dispose of the dirt since there were no other projects in the area needing fill. I proposed we spread out the dirt over an adjacent unpaved area, increasing the elevation by about 1.5 feet, and then spread gravel over it to make it usable to store containers. The client was hesitant but because I had developed a good working relationship with him, he agreed to have his technical team evaluate the proposal. I told him they might need the dirt for fill on future projects, and he could easily reuse the material then. He and his technical team agreed, and we saved $5 million dollars in trucking and disposal fees. Because of our friendly working relationship, my client worked with me to find a mutually beneficial solution. As you can see, being winsome is attractive and an asset to the project.

Be a Confidant—The ultimate benefit of being a person of peace is becoming a confidant to your client and team. You want people to trust you with issues that are hampering their performance and to be open to your counsel. "Faithful are the wounds of a friend; profuse are the kisses of an enemy" (Proverbs 27:6). We all benefit from friends and colleagues who will speak truth into our lives and correct us when we desperately need honest feedback. I am grateful for my own confidants who had the boldness to correct me when I was wrong.

I have a friend who has been a psychologist for over thirty years. She says that if people had three good friends to confide in, she would be out of a job. Sadly, many of us do not have good confidants, and our lives are diminished because of it.

Sometimes it is a challenge to find confidants within your own organization. While I was project director of a particularly difficult job, I realized I needed to develop allies whom I could confide in, so I joined a peer group[7] and hired a leadership coach. I was tempted to feel like a failure doing this, but I needed perspective from others outside my organization to develop a strategy. I was at my wits' end trying to forge a path forward on the project while keeping emotionally and physically healthy. I took some of my key issues to the peer group for their input, and the feedback I received was invaluable for completing the project. Once I was able to accept other key leaders speaking into my life, I could then become a confidant and a person of peace to them. As Proverbs 27:9 confirms, "Oil and perfume make the heart glad, and the sweetness of a friend comes from his earnest counsel."

Throughout my career, I have become a confidant without realizing it. I have had several young engineers adopt me as their mentor and bring their issues to me. I didn't realize at the time that I was acting as a confidant; I thought I was just helping them out. Years later, these engineers told me they came to me for mentoring because I was open to helping them and took the time to be with them.

CREATE JOY

You spend most of your week at work, so why not make it a place where you, your colleagues, and your employees want to be? As manager of the project, you determine the culture of your workplace. Don't be like my colleague who spends most of his time being irritated and thinks all people suck. His negative attitude poisons every place he works. Instead, you can choose to create joy on your project.

> AS MANAGER OF THE PROJECT, YOU DETERMINE THE CULTURE OF YOUR WORKPLACE.

You and your team have good reason to be joyful because your hard work produces projects that improve people's lives and serve the greater community. Enjoy your relationships with your teammates, clients, and inspectors. I still have fond memories of the teams I worked with over the years, and whenever I see any of my former colleagues, I am reminded of the joy and camaraderie of persevering through difficult projects.

CONCLUSION

Relationships are your biggest asset and will give you joy and save you when you are in trouble. Valuing relationships is not being a pushover when conflict comes. You can still be assertive in your position, protect your financial results, and stand by what you have built. In some industries, being a bully by short paying subcontractors, terminating purchase orders for convenience, and manipulating clients for the best results may be perceived as a good outcome. But you will burn all your bridges with your subs, vendors, and clients. When you go to bid another project, you will get only high quotes from subs. Clients may not even invite you to bid future projects. It takes incredible strength to be kind and keep your emotions and ego in check to complete your project successfully. Relationships are the key to success now and on the next project; therefore, invest in building and maintaining your relationships.

KEY ACTION ITEMS

1. **Genuinely Love People**—Are you demonstrating your love for others by wanting what is best for them in their careers and personal lives? Be kind for the sake of being kind. Especially show kindness to those below you in the org chart and the administrative gatekeepers to your clients. Empathize with others and realize your client and team have problems outside of work that impact the project.

2. **Build Effective Relationships**—Build relationships by applying the Golden Rule, treating others—employees, clients, and executives—how you want to be treated. Calendarize lunches and time for unofficial business visits. Play sports together if you can. If you don't play sports, plan to attend an event together outside of work. Make deposits of trust in your relationships. Stay in relationship with difficult subs and vendors by being professional and making timely payments.

3. **Be a Person of Peace**—Become that person others want to come and talk to. Be a safe person by controlling your anger. Strive to be approachable by keeping your door open to talk with people and speak gracious words. Be winsome and friendly. Be someone others actually enjoy being with and working with, even when you're solving problems together. Become a confidant to your client and

teammates. Provide earnest counsel and receive it from friends who care about you.

4. **Create Joy**—Finally, create joy in your project. Joy and leadership start at the top. You have a tremendous opportunity to lead and help make others successful as you build projects that you could never accomplish on your own. Make your project joyful!

CHAPTER 6

KNOW HOW TO NEGOTIATE

*I, wisdom, dwell with prudence, and I find knowledge
and discretion.*

PROVERBS 8:12

On one of my largest and most difficult projects, I needed to negotiate a settlement where our total claims and requests for changes were over $180 million. I had already won a dispute hearing on merit for the largest claim, and my client was now motivated to negotiate. But how could I be successful in my negotiations? I didn't feel that I had the training or authority to negotiate, and I wasn't confident I knew what the value of a good settlement would be. I spent months getting ready to negotiate and pulled in executives from my partners to help determine what "good" would look like in a settlement. Even though I was the one doing the negotiations, I built a team behind me that gave me confidence to negotiate from a position of strength.

My negotiation was a success. We ended up settling for well in excess of $100 million without going to court and paying lawyers millions of dollars for litigation. A true win!

Negotiations can bring excitement, anxiety, and dread. Executives often get involved and set high expectations for revenue recovery that are not tied to reality. You may see negotiations as a lose-lose proposition because no matter how they turn out, you fear that another manager could have done better. Or as one of my executives admonished me whenever we had an opportunity to get paid for a change in work, "Don't be a chump!"

We have all experienced situations where we wish we had negotiated better with better outcomes. This chapter will demystify negotiating and provide a roadmap for you to prepare for negotiations. We will review different models of negotiating, examine what type of negotiator you are, and give you tools to understand your counterpart's negotiation style. We will examine *prudence* and *discretion*, which are the essence of ancient wisdom for speaking and listening. Next, we will walk through the steps to prepare for negotiations. And finally, we will identify best practices in negotiating.

NEGOTIATIONS AND APPROACHES TO CONFLICT

All of life is a negotiation. You started negotiating as a toddler to see if you could get your way with your parents: "Cookie first, then vegetables." We negotiate with our internet provider, our children, our spouse, and contractors working on our house. Frequently, we're surprised to find ourselves in a negotiation we have not prepared for. Some of us thrive on negotiations, while others of us completely avoid them because they are so uncomfortable.

ALL OF LIFE IS A NEGOTIATION.

When our oldest child was a senior in high school, my wife and I decided to help him purchase a car. We were paying for it, and he would pay us back. We had picked out the car from a local dealer and had settled on the price. When we went with our son to pick up the car, the dealer started to renegotiate the price. I wanted to walk away from the deal, but my son and wife were already emotionally involved and didn't want to leave without the car. I lost that negotiation, and it cost me an extra five hundred dollars. I learned two things that day: All negotiations are emotional and rarely rational, and I need to be better prepared and be ready to walk away.

How do you approach negotiations? Is there always a clear winner and loser? Do you ask for more so that your client can feel good about driving down your price during negotiations? Do you try to first identify the top three things you and your client agree on and then move on from there? Should you compromise and split the difference? Or do you simply avoid conflict inherent in negotiations?

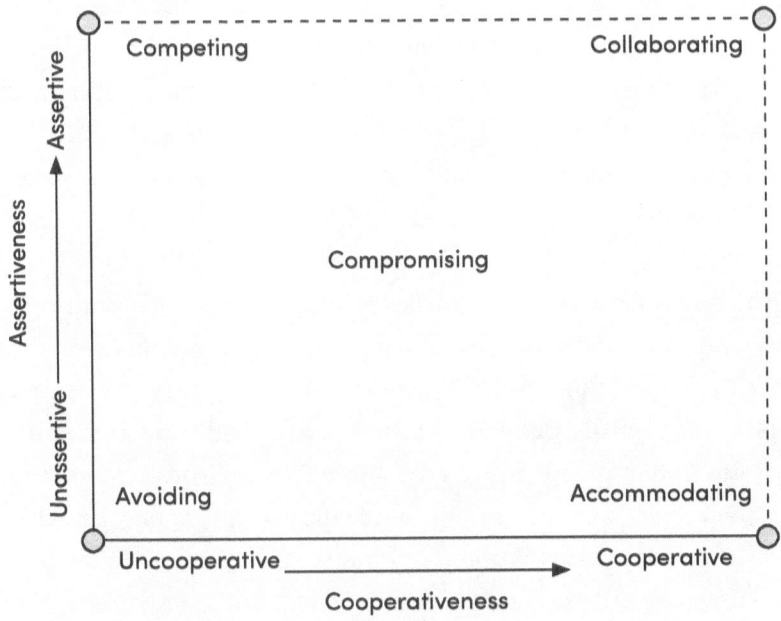

Figure 6.1–Five Conflict Handling Modes

Kenneth Thomas and Ralph Kilmann developed the Thomas-Kilmann Conflict Mode Instrument, which identifies five different ways to handle conflict, as shown in Figure 6.1 above.[8] The x-axis measures Cooperativeness, which is your investment in satisfying the other person's concerns. As cooperativeness increases, behavior moves from Uncooperative to Cooperative. The y-axis measures Assertiveness, which is the amount of energy you put into satisfying your own concerns. Starting at the bottom of the y-axis, Unassertive behavior moves up to Assertive behavior. There are five different ways people deal with conflict and negotiations: Competing, Accommodating, Avoiding, Collaborating, and Compromising.[9]

A competing person is one who is assertive and uncooperative. All their energy goes into satisfying their own goals. These are usually type A managers, and their behavior can come across as offensive in negotiations. The competing person will use whatever power is necessary to win. One of my executives exhibited this behavior and came across as a bully in negotiations with the client. The client tolerated his behavior, but the negotiations went nowhere. The client ended the meeting with, "We will think about it," which meant they were done and didn't want to deal with him again. You can be a competing person and have success in a negotiation; you just need to pick your battles and not shame your client.

The opposite of competing is avoiding. This person is both unassertive and uncooperative. They don't pursue their own goals or their client's goals. They just want to avoid conflict and sidestep issues or postpone them until a better time to negotiate. I had another executive who was conflict averse and always busied himself on his computer when there was conflict in meetings. He didn't want to engage, which left his own people exposed and open to attack. Obviously, avoiding often hinders positive negotiations; however, there are times when you may choose to diplomatically avoid a conflict until you are ready to engage.

Accommodating is unassertive and cooperative. This person is a client pleaser and is willing to sacrifice his own concerns to meet his client's desires. Many designers and architects exhibit this behavior because they believe it is necessary to gain the client's approval and be awarded the next job. If you're always accommodating, however, you will be taken advantage of and may grow to resent those you yield to.

Collaborating is both assertive and cooperative. A collaborating negotiator works with the client to find a solution that satisfies both parties, where both can claim a win in the negotiations. This requires some analytical skills to dig into the details and determine the underlying issues that are important to both parties. On a critical issue where I believed I was absolutely correct, my client chose to collaborate and told me how to recalculate the damages so he could get his board's approval. I didn't understand what he was saying. At first, I thought he was saying "No!" But he was just telling me to calculate the damages differently. Once I did, his board approved the change, and we received a $500,000 change order.

Compromising is being somewhat assertive and cooperative. It is splitting the difference both in price and goals. Compromising gives up more than competing, but less than accommodating. There are some issues where it is not worth the energy to obtain all your goals. In these cases, you can claim a win when the client merits your argument and is willing to pay half of your costs. But you need to make sure you actually know your costs before you settle. I have heard numerous complaints from executives that their project managers made agreements on what they *thought* were good deals, but they had no idea of their actual costs and ended up losing money.

So, what type of negotiator are you? What is your primary mode of conflict? And just as important, what is your client's mode of conflict? I encourage you to take the Thomas-Kilmann Instrument assessment tool online and read the strengths and weaknesses of each mode or type of negotiator.[10] You may find that you use all the modes in your work, but, like personality traits, you will have one dominant mode for negotiating.

PRACTICE PRUDENCE AND DISCRETION

Prudence and discretion are at the heart of negotiations and the key to having wisdom. "I, wisdom, dwell with prudence, and I find knowledge and discretion" (Proverbs 8:12). Prudence helps us take the right steps at the right time in the right way. It is knowing what to say and when to speak. Discretion is the ability to examine a path and avoid following one that leads to destruction. It results from practicing wisdom and knowing how to stay out of trouble. Discretion is also knowing when to keep your mouth shut. Both prudence and discretion are needed in negotiations.

Discretion—Since all negotiations can be emotional and at times irrational, it is often difficult to control what comes out of our mouths. Proverbs 17:27 states, "Whoever restrains his words has knowledge, and he who has a cool spirit is a man of understanding." At the start of a negotiation, we are tempted to let people know how strong our position is and how smart we are. This doesn't help the negotiations and can polarize the parties. Often, the wisest way to demonstrate your intelligence is to stay quiet. You always want the other side to go first and make an offer for settlement. Their offer may be better than what you were willing to settle for.

It is especially important to remain silent when you are unsure about the strength of your position. I was working with my drainage manager on the merit of his claim. He was ready to give up, but I told him to review the standard plans one more time to see if we could find an argument to support our position. He found a document that showed our original plan was acceptable and the client's direction to change to a more expensive type of inlet was not required by the standards. We presented this new evidence to the client and waited for him to make an offer. In the end, we settled for $500,000! If we had gone first in the negotiation, we would have been happy with half that amount. Silence is powerful in negotiations. Become comfortable with silence. Remember, "The wise lay up knowledge, but the mouth of a fool brings ruin near" (Proverbs 10:14).

> ## SILENCE IS POWERFUL IN NEGOTIATIONS. BECOME COMFORTABLE WITH SILENCE.

Prudence—Learn to say the right thing at the right time to the right audience. We often make the mistake of negotiating with someone who doesn't have the authority to settle, which only exposes our position to be used against us later.

One project controls specialist kept trying to engage me in technical arguments of merit in front of the manager I would soon be negotiating with. I told the specialist that our position was clearly laid out in our letters and design submittals, and there was nothing more to discuss. I didn't reveal my position, and we later ended up settling this issue at our cost for doing the extra work.

To have prudence is to be thoughtful and to think ahead before you enter negotiations. Proverbs 15:23 states, "To make an apt answer is a joy to a man, and a word in season, how good it is!" It is very rewarding to turn someone to your side and have them end the negotiation by agreeing with your position.

I negotiated a very large owner-caused delay claim with one of the owner's executives. We had added to the ledger our requests for change orders, and he built up his damages against us that would reduce our claim by millions of dollars. He assessed sixty days of liquidated damages at approximately $100,000/day, for a total damage of $6 million. A year earlier, I had submitted a request for sixty additional days of non-compensated time for weather days. I reminded him that we did this, and he said they had denied it. I produced a letter from the owner acknowledging merit for thirty days, and he agreed to reduce the damages by $3 million. With prudence and having the right answer at the right time with the right person, I increased our settlement by $3 million.

PLAN YOUR STEPS

It is impossible to be prudent and show discretion if you don't plan out your steps for the negotiation. "The simple believes everything, but the prudent gives thought to his steps" (Proverbs 14:15). You cannot walk into a negotiation without a game plan. You will need to (1) gather your team to negotiate, (2) identify your goal for the negotiation, (3) prepare emotionally for the negotiation, and (4) script your quantitative questions.

Gather Your Team—You need a team to prepare for negotiations. You will never have perfect clarity by yourself. Your team will help identify the different facets of what you want out of the negotiation and how best to pursue it. Proverbs 24:5–6 says, "A wise man is full of strength, and a man of knowledge enhances his might, for by wise guidance you can wage your war, and in abundance of counselors there is victory."

> YOU WILL NEVER HAVE PERFECT CLARITY BY YOURSELF.

You also need team members to attend the negotiation to listen, read body language, and take notes. (We will expand on this later in the chapter.) When you have a team, they help keep you accountable to be prepared before you go into negotiations. My deputy project manager always scheduled pre-meetings with me before we met with the client to review our claims. He wanted to make sure we were on the same page, and we would then decide who would take the lead on each issue.

Don't think you are the only one who can negotiate changes with the client. I had my discipline managers negotiate change orders with their counterparts. They knew the cost and the impact of the client's changes. I didn't have to be "the man." In a couple of situations, I negotiated outside of my knowledge of the work and forfeited some of our costs in the final change order. After that, I made sure my discipline managers identified the costs before starting negotiations.

Identify the Goal—With the help of your team, identify the best outcome of the negotiation. What do you want out of it? Some parties tell you to identify the low, mid, and high dollar amounts you want from your negotiations. This may seem wise, but once you identify a low number and write it down, you are more likely to settle at that. Spend time with your team gathering input on what the final price should be. Write down the value that you want out of negotiations.

Sometimes you can only close all your changes through a global settlement with your client. On one project, we did a bottom-up analysis evaluating the cost of each requested change order by identifying the low, middle, and high of what we thought the owner would pay based on the strength of the merit argument. Some we evaluated at 90 percent and others at 10 percent of the value of what we had requested. Unsurprisingly, the owner didn't see the issues the same way we did. He overvalued some of our risky claims and undervalued our strong claims. But through this detailed analysis, we identified the total amount we were looking for and could then negotiate for the whole settlement.

Next, identify the non-monetary items you want out of the negotiation. What are the terms for when you get paid? Can you tie the change order to being paid in thirty days? What are the terms of the settlement agreement? Are you taking on additional risk or reducing it with the language? You never want to take on an additional warranty period, for example, or admit to not meeting the criteria of the contract.

Once you identify the goal, make sure your executives buy into the goal and that you have the necessary authority to negotiate. You also need to obtain concurrence from your team so you all share the same goal.

Prepare Emotionally for Negotiations—
Recognize that negotiations are not completely rational and linear; rather, they can be emotional and irrational. There are many human factors that come into a negotiation that you could never predict. As project managers and technical people, we would like others to see the world

> **RECOGNIZE THAT NEGOTIATIONS ARE NOT COMPLETELY RATIONAL AND LINEAR.**

as we do—as perfectly ordered. But even that is a fallacy because we are asserting our emotional desires in the negotiations. So, expect the negotiations not to go as planned. Stay calm and listen.

Use your listening and observational skills to determine your client's emotions on the issue before starting negotiations. Utilize your team to help you do this. Write down or label the emotions you and your team have observed in your client. For example, your client may be hesitant to approve a change order because they're afraid you will use it as a precedent for other changes. Or your client doesn't have the authority to settle at the dollar value you want. Maybe the client is angry that you keep asking for changes. Write down your observations and say them back to the client during negotiations. This honest empathy will help build collaboration and close the issue. Once your client feels that you understand their position, they will be more likely to settle with you.

One warning—don't go into negotiations angry and vindictive. Your company may have been significantly wronged by your client, but anger and an aggressive attitude will not help you. It will make the client defensive and withdrawn. If you cannot control your emotions, have someone else negotiate. I have a very successful friend who has a huge justice factor and hates how his client's consultants harm his projects. He knows he can't hide his anger, so he has his deputies conduct negotiations.

Script Your Qualitative Questions—A qualitative question begins with the word *how* or *what*, but never with *why*. An example of a qualitative question to ask your client is, "How can I walk away from this negotiation without recovering my costs for the added work?" Notice you have now put the client in the position of solving your problem. You could have said, "I need at least $50,000 to cover my costs." Then the client would have countered your offer, and you would have settled for less.

We are not accustomed to asking qualitative questions, because we like to have the answers ourselves. That is why it is imperative to script your questions ahead of time. You could ask, "What did you think would happen when you issued the directive to increase our scope of work?" Or "How do you expect us to keep funding the job when you will not execute a change order?" Or "What does good look like? How can we solve this issue?" The best question to use in a negotiation is, "How am I supposed to accept that?" This question puts the onus back on the client to solve your problem.

Brainstorm with your team members what open-ended *how* and *what* questions you want to ask. Write your questions out and be ready to use them. But after asking your questions, stay quiet. Let the client answer them. Be patient and learn to be comfortable with uncomfortable silence.

> **LEARN TO BE COMFORTABLE WITH UNCOMFORTABLE SILENCE.**

NEGOTIATE WITH CONFIDENCE

Thousands of books have been written on how to negotiate. In this section, I will cover some of the advice I have found most helpful. The best book I have read on negotiating is *Never Split the Difference* by Chris Voss.[11] For more than fifteen years, he was a lead hostage negotiator for the FBI and developed several effective negotiating techniques. I have used many of his tips in my own negotiations, and I will highlight here those transferable to project management.

Bring a Team to Listen and Learn—As engineers and project managers, we spend a lot of time postulating what the client's position is and then make elaborate plans to counter their position. The problem is that our projections are usually wrong and get us locked into an erroneous position that hurts our end result.

As a prime contractor, I support subcontractors' claims and negotiations with my client. In one negotiation, I watched a designer spend all their time beating the dead horse that they were damaged. The client had already conceded they were damaged. He just needed the costs backed up, which the designer could not do. So, after wasting several days (and many hours of expensive lawyer fees!), they finally began negotiating the dollar amount.

You really don't know the client's position unless they tell you. So, treat negotiations as discovery. Proverbs 18:13 states, "If one gives an answer before he hears, it is his folly and shame." If you are primarily doing the speaking, it is difficult for you to listen with the intent of discovering the real position behind your client's words. You need other people in the room or listening virtually. They are not there to talk but to listen and observe body language. Have a key person take notes and then debrief afterward. If you don't have a woman on your team in the negotiations, you won't pick up on all the nonverbal communications. Women have great intuition, insight, and emotional intelligence. Bring them to the negotiating table, and they will be an asset to your team.

I made it a rule to never negotiate on my own. When I am presenting, I'm thinking about what I am going to say next and may miss important clues. Even in phone conversations, I put the phone on speaker so another member of my team can listen in and take notes. Realize, too, that negotiations don't start when you are finally talking dollars. Negotiations start as soon as there is an issue that is going to cost more money.

On one of my projects, I had a large, complex issue where both parties were firmly set in their opposing positions. During one executive partnering session, I asked the owner what they needed to reach a settlement. They requested bringing in a third party, per the contract, to decide because it was too big of an issue. With that insight, we focused our energy on preparing for a third-party dispute review board. We knew there would be no negotiations if we didn't win a favorable decision from the board. By directly asking a question, my team knew where to focus our resources to win.

Let the Other Side Go First—If possible, let your client's representative go first in negotiations. You may be disappointed by their first offer, but you also may be surprised. The worst thing to do in negotiations is to negotiate against yourself by cutting your asking price before starting negotiations. You may feel you don't have a strong position in your claim or proposed change order. But the very fact that your client is talking to you about it and entering negotiations tells you they have something to lose. That is why they are negotiating.

I am always surprised by how owners evaluate change orders. They have a different view of risk than we do and are motivated to solve that risk and negotiate changes. If they fully understand the proposed change order, they will argue more strongly for their case and reduced cost. If they don't understand it and see the proposed change order as a looming risk, they will offer more money to settle now to eliminate the unknown risk.

I was recently talking to an owner's rep on a project we closed out several years ago. I thanked him for being a good partner in reaching a settlement. He said, "I had to resolve the issues because the risks were too large to let it go forward." He knew he had a greater risk of increased costs if the claim went to court.

A great way to deepen your understanding of your client's position is to state back what they just said in different words. For example, your client says, "I only see this change order valued at $100,000. I don't see merit in your $500,000 request." You don't ask why. You don't ask them to support their calculations. You don't ask to see their breakdown. You just say, "So, you evaluate this change order at $100,000?" Let them explain why they see it that way. You can learn a lot and avoid coming across as aggressive by simply repeating back to your client what they said.

I was negotiating a change order on a complex geotechnical issue and "mirrored"[12] back my client's statements until he realized, after restating his position several times, that there was no merit to what he was saying. We later agreed to a change order.

Stay Flexible and Slow It Down—As I've mentioned earlier, don't get locked into your position and theories of what the other party is thinking. Keep them as hypotheses and be ready to change your mind quickly. Proverbs 20:5 states, "The purpose in a man's heart is like deep water, but a man of understanding will draw it out." I spent three months negotiating a global settlement valued at over $100 million. The negotiations provided a constant revelation of my client's position and their evaluation of all the requested change orders. I had to be patient and flexible. I had to be willing to give up on changes I thought had strong entitlement and embrace the weaker changes my client evaluated favorably.

When you are in a negotiation, don't think you must have a quick resolution. Take baby steps in moving toward a resolution and then schedule another time to meet. Go slow and listen. If you don't have an answer to the client's arguments, take a break and query your team.

GO SLOW AND LISTEN.

As you slow down the negotiations, seek to understand what type of negotiator your client is. Are they competing or avoiding? Are they accommodating or collaborating? Are they assertive or cooperative? Once you understand their mode of negotiating, you will know better how to bring the negotiations to a close. Some negotiators are analytical and cannot make a decision until they closely examine all the details of the settlement. If you are dealing with analytical negotiators (as most engineers are), you must give them time to arrive at their number.

Recognize Emotional Blocks to Reaching a Settlement—As we discussed, negotiations are often emotional and not rational. Your client brings their emotions to the table. Recognize that there may be some emotional block to reaching a settlement that you need to help solve by how you craft the change order. What are their fears of moving forward?

On one project, I was trying to implement an easier administrative process for documenting design changes to approved plans. The owner had a cumbersome process that took a week to get through a change. I was left with the option of stopping work or doing it at risk. So, I began negotiating with the owner to implement Field Design Changes (FDC) to document the change and obtain the owner's concurrence within four hours to move forward in construction. But he was hesitant to approve it. I asked why, and he said he thought we would abuse the process and then blame him for obstructing the work. I assured him that it was a simple administrative process, and if they denied the FDC, we would quickly move to an official design change with the engineer of record's approval. I also reassured him that we didn't want to take the risk of doing the work without his approval. After the job was completed, the owner admitted he was surprised by how well the change worked and that we didn't abuse the process. Maybe on the next project he will trust me more.

Seek to understand the constraints your counterpart has in negotiations. What is driving their desire to negotiate? Once you understand their constraints, you are on your way to reaching a settlement.

Embrace the Power of "No"—There was a famous Southern California pastor who emphasized positive thinking. He used to say, "Embrace the possibility of 'Yes!'" Well, in negotiations, the power is not in "Yes!" but in "No!" Once you hear a clear "no," you can take comfort in knowing that you are closer to a settlement because this is the real start of negotiations. You want to avoid a weak "yes" or "I will think about it and get back to you." "No" means that together you can now move forward to the real issues.

You also need to discern through open-ended questions what "no" means. Does it mean they don't have the money to issue the change? Does it mean they don't have the authority to make the change? Does it mean they can't go to their board of directors for two months to get approval to issue the change? Or does it mean they want to pay less for the change? Find out what is driving the "no," and you can close the negotiation.

Finally, remember the warning of Proverbs 20:14: "'Bad, bad,' says the buyer, but when he goes away, then he boasts." Your client may be saying "No" as a negotiating tactic to get a greater reduction on the cost of the change.

Persuasion and Walking Away from the Table—"With patience a ruler may be persuaded, and a soft tongue will break a bone" (Proverbs 25:15). Don't forget that you can be assertive and persuasive with a soft voice. Chris Voss refers to his negotiating voice as an FM

> **DON'T FORGET THAT YOU CAN BE ASSERTIVE AND PERSUASIVE WITH A SOFT VOICE.**

DJ voice[13]—deep and reassuring. He uses this voice to calm down terrorists in critical situations. You, too, can use this soft, comforting voice to be persuasive. Ancient wisdom teaches that *how* something is said is of equal importance to *what* is said: "The wise of heart is called discerning, and sweetness of speech increases persuasiveness" (Proverbs 16:21). Remember to keep your speech sweet.

Another tactic to be persuasive in your negotiations is to first identify all the negative attributes the owner may be assigning to you. By stating them first, you take away the sting and cause the owner to start defending your actions. For example, you could say, "I know you think our work is lacking, that it's late, and our requested change orders are too highly priced." The owner would then say in your defense, "Your work is good, and we are close to finishing the project." Once you get rid of the negative unspoken accusations, you can move forward to a settlement.

In addition, never feel pressure to settle. Know that you can walk away from the table. When you are willing to walk, you actually have incredible power in your negotiations.

After I successfully completed a large project and shepherded the claims through to win a merit decision from a third party, I told my senior executives I was leaving. If they wanted to use me to close the settlement, they needed to bring me on as a consultant and pay me my project bonus. I was burned out on this long and difficult project, and I was completely willing to walk. They ended up giving me everything I asked for without negotiating me down.

Closing the Deal—Once you agree on dollars in the settlement, don't end negotiations until you've settled on the final language in the executed agreement or change order. Deadlines can be useful in closing the deal. Use them to help bring the negotiations to a close, but don't be held hostage to them. You can still stay flexible if needed.

Once while I was working on a global settlement for a large project, we were running out of time before we had to file a lawsuit or lose our rights. I used this deadline with my owner to write a term sheet that defined the low and high values of possible settlements. This term sheet was then our guiding document to complete the negotiations.

You have a much better chance of closing the deal if your client owns the deal. On the same project for which we created a term sheet, my client was the first one to say the number we would settle on. I waited for him to say it two more times before I concurred. He then had ownership of the deal and worked with the lawyers and his staff to get a settlement agreement written and executed.

After you agree to the financial terms, talk about the non-monetary terms like when payment is received and any other items that will reduce your risk in the settlement.

CONCLUSION

As a project manager, you will need to negotiate change orders. Start preparing now. From the first day of the project, prepare for negotiations by building trust with your client and discerning how they deal with conflict and proposed changes on your project. Realize you don't need to be alone in negotiations and that there is power in a team approach. Remember, "The way of a fool is right in his own eyes, but a wise man listens to advice" (Proverbs 12:15). Listen to your team!

KEY ACTION ITEMS

1. **Recognize Your Default Conflict Mode in Negotiations**—Are you *competing, accommodating, avoiding, collaborating,* or *compromising?* Are you trying to preserve relationships and avoid conflict, or are you putting all your energy into accomplishing your goals regardless of others? There is no wrong answer, but do a self-evaluation and shore up your negotiations with team members of different strengths.

2. **Practice Prudence and Discretion**—All negotiation tactics and planning can be reduced to prudence and discretion. Discretion is staying quiet and listening. Prudence is saying the right thing at the right time to the right audience. The ancients knew that this was the essence of wisdom: "I, wisdom, dwell with prudence, and I find knowledge and discretion" (Proverbs 8:12). The only way to be prudent and stay quiet is to prepare for negotiations.

3. **Plan Your Steps**—You will not have successful negotiations if you do not take the time to plan. Prepare for negotiations by gathering your team, identifying your goals (financial and contractual), preparing emotionally to engage in negotiations, and scripting your qualitative questions. Write on one sheet of paper your high goal, the makeup of your team, your strengths in merit, and the open-ended qualitative questions (How? What? When?).

4. **Negotiate with Confidence**—There are multiple tactics and strategies to negotiating. First, don't do it alone—bring a team to listen and learn during negotiations. Always let the other side go first. Stay flexible and slow down the negotiations so you can learn what the real issues are to reaching a settlement. Embrace the strong "no" that comes from the other side of the table. You are now close to reaching a deal. Close the deal by letting your client state the settlement amount first. They will then be committed to shepherding the settlement through to the end.

5. **Finally, a Warning**—Don't demand justice because you have been financially damaged by your client or their representatives. If you show anger early on in negotiations, you will fail. You may be completely contractually correct in your position, but at the end of the day, realize your goal is to successfully close out your negotiations and move on to the next job. Remember to be persuasive and not angry. "The heart of the wise makes his speech judicious and adds persuasiveness to his lips" (Proverbs 16:23).

CHAPTER 7

TRACK YOUR PERFORMANCE

*Know well the condition of your flocks, and give attention
to your herds, for riches do not last forever; and does a
crown endure to all generations?*

In 1997, I attended my first Estimated Cost at Completion (ECAC) meeting for an $800 million toll road. I didn't know anything about tracking and reporting cost, and I was overwhelmed by the thousands of cost codes broken down by discipline and location of work. The costs were then further categorized by type of cost—equipment, material, subcontractor, and labor. I remember thinking, "How can anyone keep track of this massive cost report?" I have since learned that what you don't regularly track and review, you have no control over, and the consequences will chase you down and overtake your life. Tracking progress, cost, and revenue—which then produces profit—is the mortar of project management that holds the project together. Once I understood that I was responsible for my area of the cost report, I tracked it and strategized how to reduce my budgeted costs from $10 million to $9 million.

The ancients knew that wealth did not endure, and future income was not guaranteed. They instructed those in an agrarian society to "know well the condition of your flocks, and give attention to your herds." They needed to pay attention to their source of income. If trouble developed with their livestock, it was best to identify it early, before sickness spread through the whole herd. We are to heed this sage advice and pay attention to our project costs and projections so when things go wrong (and they always do), we have time to jump sideways and address the cost overruns before they destroy the whole project.

This chapter will explore the wisdom and practices needed to track the performance of your project. We will discuss how to determine the appropriate level of detail to break down your project. From this detail, we will examine how to track your costs and the report you want to generate to properly evaluate your production, cost, and profit. Next, we will look at the schedule for your project and the specific activities you need to track and update monthly. Then we'll dive into costs, revenue, and project reporting for estimated cost at completion. Finally, we will discuss the need to track cash flow and accounts receivable.

> **BE PREPARED TO PUT IN THE TIME TO PLAN, BUDGET, AND SCHEDULE YOUR PROJECT.**

Tracking your performance may seem overwhelming, but once you develop effective systems and break the project down into bite-sized pieces, you can stay on top of the schedule and costs. But it is hard work. Proverbs 20:4 states, "The sluggard does not plow in the autumn; he will seek at harvest and have nothing." Be prepared to put in the time to plan, budget, and schedule your project. You will then have a great harvest of profit at the end of the project.

WORK BREAKDOWN STRUCTURE

You probably have an intuitive idea of the larger buckets or headings of the type of work in your project, but at what level do you break down the project to correctly track cost, schedule, and production? This detail is your Work Breakdown Structure (WBS). Many clients will ask for it because they want to use your WBS as a means for payment and verifying production.

In building a simple two-span bridge over a highway, for example, the four large headings of work are foundations, substructure, super-structure, and miscellaneous finishes. If the cost of the bridge is esti-mated at $5 million, the breakdown would be:

Foundations	$1,000,000
Substructure	$750,000
Superstructure	$2,500,000
Misc Finishes	$750,000

You won't have enough control over costs to track performance in these large buckets, so the next action is to decide how much further to break down the activities and their budgets. But be careful not to go overboard and divide the work into too many activities. For example, the further breakdown of foundations on that two-span bridge would be the following:

Foundations	
Abutments	
Install Shoring	
Excavate abutments	
Drive Piles	
Form, Pour and Strip Pile Caps	
Fill, Final Grading	
Columns	
Install Shoring	
Excavate	
Drive Piles	

For each of these items, there would be costs for labor, equipment, permanent materials (concrete and steel), and subcontractors. The project engineer is responsible for assigning the costs to the proper codes in the cost report. If a cost is miscoded, it should be reclassified to the appropriate cost code. This will provide accurate data for management reviews and a true cost basis for future bids.

For your project, the breakdown may look different. No matter what your project is, ask yourself, "Where do I have the best ability to control my costs?" In construction, it is usually in your self-performed or in-house labor. The other costs of permanent materials, subcontractors, and equipment are mostly fixed once you have bid and won the project. What are the primary costs you can control through proper tracking and management? Address these items at the level of detail necessary to control costs. In some cases, your own internal overhead (engineers, project managers, and superintendents) may be too costly and cause the project and your company to lose money. What isn't tracked will naturally grow and end up hurting your project. Without a clear work breakdown structure, you will see your cost magically grow beyond your budget.

> WITHOUT A CLEAR WORK BREAKDOWN STRUCTURE, YOU WILL SEE YOUR COST MAGICALLY GROW BEYOND YOUR BUDGET.

Proverbs 18:9 warns, "Whoever is slack in his work is a brother to him who destroys." Don't be shortsighted in developing the details to track your project. Spend time weekly reviewing your production rates and associated costs. On one complicated bridge project, we were getting our butts kicked, losing time and money forming the hinges (where one bridge span joined another span). We had to stop what we were doing and reevaluate our means and methods. We built three-dimensional computer-aided design and drafting (CADD) models with the primary superintendent responsible for the work. Based on the modeling, he decided to construct form templates for the hinge and then place the rebar around the form. Once we started utilizing these templates, our costs went down and production went up. We fabricated hinges with 200,000 pounds of rebar on the ground and flew them into place with our large cranes. This trimmed our schedule by two weeks for each span.

SCHEDULE

In managing your project, you cannot overestimate the importance of developing a schedule that is accurate, properly detailed, and logically ties activities to subsequent work. For example, when building a house, the foundation is poured before framing, roofing, adding drywall, and installing final plumbing and electrical fixtures. But how long will each activity take, and what are the logical ties between each item of work? In any project, many activities are sequential and need to be finished before the next piece of work begins. These logically connected finish-start activities can become part of the project's critical path. On the other hand, many activities or procurements can be completed concurrently with other activities. Most delays in home building, for example, are due to long procurements for kitchen cabinets, fixtures, and enclosed appliances. These procurements can start while constructing the foundation so they are on-site and ready to be installed once the kitchen construction has progressed.

The problem with creating and managing your project schedule is that many technicians who know how to operate the scheduling software (Primavera 6, Microsoft Project, etc.) don't know what it takes to actually construct the project; therefore, as project manager, you can't just delegate creating your schedule to technicians. You need to be involved in identifying the detailed activities and logical predecessors and successors in your schedule. Next, you need to verify that the durations are realistic and are a proper basis for managing schedule delays potentially caused by your subcontractors or client. Proverbs 24:27 states, "Prepare your work outside; get everything ready for yourself in the field, and after that build your house." Spend the necessary time to create your schedule activities, estimate the durations, and define the logic ties (predecessors and successors) to each activity.

Most project managers underestimate the time it takes to plan their project accurately. They worry that they need to start the project right away, or they will fall behind. This is a critical error. You need to take the time to create a good plan for your project. Many project managers also fail to plan out their deliverables or establish milestones they want to reach and get paid for by their client. Preconstruction services that include permits, shop drawings, long-term procurements, insurance certificates, and early submittals are critical activities to start your project well. Plan for these items and tie revenue/billings for this early work and mobilization to the project.

My colleague Dan, who designs apps, always begins with the final product in mind. His team will storyboard all the menus in the apps and which subsequent menu will pop up when the user clicks on it. He then gets the client to sign off on all these menus before writing a single line of code. This eliminates changes in the middle of programming. He also ties a portion of the total payment to this early engineering activity before coding is started.

Regarding revenue, when do you want to get paid for your project? Are there early deliverables or milestones you want to receive payment for so you don't have cash flow problems? Break down your schedule to track activities that are tied to revenue. You don't need to include minor activities for every item on your project. You can build hammocks (smaller tasks combined into larger, more manageable items) into your schedule to cover this work. If, however, there are deliverables in your contract that the client requires to be verified for payment, put these submittals in your schedule.

On many of the large projects I have worked on, the client had onerous requirements limiting each activity in the schedule to a $250,000 value. For example, for a single-day monolithic placement of concrete for a soffit and stem on a bridge that cost $1 million, we had to use four schedule activities and then status them. These requirements are unrealistic and unhelpful. Be careful not to include minor work activities in your schedule that will then need to be tracked in your monthly progress updates submitted to your client.

Know the critical path in your schedule. On the cable-stayed bridge project, installation of the large, drilled shafts that supported the bents/columns for the bridge was delayed. We couldn't mitigate the delays by starting on the superstructure because we needed the foundations first. The schedule showed the critical path going through the foundations,

> **KNOW THE CRITICAL PATH IN YOUR SCHEDULE.**

so we managed this work very closely, pushed hard to get started, and then accelerated the drilled shaft activities to avoid a critical path delay.

Besides creating a proper baseline schedule for your project, updating your progress in your monthly schedule with the actual date the work was performed is essential to successful project management. These monthly submittals can serve as contemporaneous records if you experience active interference and direction from your client that delays the project. Usually, you can only obtain a compensable delay change order if your client's directions delayed the critical path. You cannot go back and adjust your logic and schedule activities to create a critical path delay. You can only rely on your monthly updates. Therefore, review your monthly submittals to verify they are accurate and put in the necessary narratives on what is causing delays. All of this may be used for or against you in the future.

On one project, I submitted a large delay claim against the owner seeking a compensable delay change order of around $130,000 per day. The monthly schedule updates consistently showed the critical path for constructing the bridge had not changed. Then a key supplier rescinded their subcontract for designing and fabricating a $3 million bridge component. This had the potential to become the critical path for completing the project and put my large owner-caused delay claim in jeopardy. So what did I do? I quickly jumped sideways. I re-procured the fabrication with another supplier while working out a change order to keep my current supplier on board to complete the design. I also reserved all rights to pursue him later for damages. Lesson learned—know your critical path and manage your monthly updates.

COSTS

Early in my project management experience, I made the mistake of equating costs with revenue. At the time, I was managing small design projects with a budget of approximately $200,000. I had four distinct design submittals, and I had divided the budget up for each deliverable. I thought that with each submittal, my costs were matching what I was invoicing. I was completely wrong and had cost overruns at the end of the project. In design, we say that completing the last 10 percent of the work takes 90 percent of the effort. Now that isn't completely accurate, but every project takes longer and costs more than you think. If I had tracked my costs and not revenue, I could have planned to mitigate these overruns.

Do you know your costs? Cost is whatever you are paying in equipment, labor, materials, and subcontractors to perform the work. How do you know your costs are accurate? What is your estimated profit? How much remaining costs do you have? Did you include a contingency in your budget? If you don't know the answers to these questions, you are not attuned to the costs of your project. It is critical to manage your costs. Proverbs 10:4 states, "A slack hand causes poverty, but the hand of the diligent makes rich." Do not be slack in tracking and projecting your costs. Be attentive and plan to track them according to the buckets you set up in your work breakdown structure.

Don't let yourself be deceived in managing your costs. When I was project manager for a $500 million transit project in Los Angeles, we divided the new eight-mile rail line into reaches or segments. Reach 1 was the most demanding with a cut-and-cover tunnel, and I had no idea what the actual costs were. Why? Because the project engineer was three to four months behind in processing invoices from subcontractors and suppliers. I visited his office in the field and sat with him until he entered all the invoices into our cost management software. On another large project, I had the opposite problem. Every time I reviewed the costs with the segment manager, he projected hundreds of thousands of dollars in costs after the majority of the work had been completed. I asked him why, and he explained that two of his subcontractors were notoriously late submitting invoices for their work, and he was planning for those costs. As project manager, you must know if your cost report accurately includes current costs and that all invoices are up to date.

Do not purposefully deceive or manipulate your costs to appear to have better results. The ancient world was primarily an agrarian economy, and merchants would sell grain and produce based on the weight of the commodities. But some unscrupulous people would cheat and modify the weights or scales to their advantage. The ancient wise men warned against this: "A false balance is an abomination to the Lord, but a just weight is his delight" (Proverbs 11:1). Don't deceive others for your advantage. Over the years, I knew many project managers who were under great pressure to make small compromises in recording costs. You may be asked to do this on your projects. Don't succumb to the temptation. Be clean and above reproach in reporting your costs, and let your executives decide if they want to change what they report for their company financials. Proverbs 26:28 succinctly states the true motivation of deception: "A lying tongue hates its victims, and a flattering mouth works ruin." One of my colleagues had a flattering tongue when it came to accurately reporting costs. He overestimated revenue to offset his costs and was eventually found out and let go.

> **BE CLEAN AND ABOVE REPROACH IN REPORTING YOUR COSTS.**

REVENUE

Revenue is accounts receivable from your client. It is being paid for your work. In managing projects, you set up your overall budget based on the revenue you will receive. You don't work for free or make donations to your clients. My colleagues have repeatedly said, "If I want to lose money, I would rather do it on a beach in Mexico than working this hard for an owner who doesn't pay." Your projected revenue should be the value in your contract, purchase order, or subcontract. Once the contract is executed, you can then assign revenue to the project and start work.

But what about the temptation to recognize soft revenue (projected change orders or claims against your client)? When is it prudent to increase your budget based on a verbal commitment from your client to pay for a change? What if it is not a verbal commitment, but you have very high confidence in the merit of your requested change order? This, indeed, is a slippery slope that once started down is very difficult to stop. Proverbs 15:27 warns, "Whoever is greedy for unjust gain troubles his own household."

Some companies have rules in place for early recognition of soft revenue. Others do not. After being burned over the years by verbal commitments that were not followed by executed change orders, I only recognize revenue once I have a signed change order. This keeps me from overpromising and underdelivering. It is always better to underpromise and overdeliver.

Beware of recognizing revenue from claims submitted to the owner before the claim is settled. All soft revenue should be tracked with a risk/opportunity sheet and not treated as actual revenue unless a change order has been executed. Notice that risk is included with opportunities. Opportunities are the project manager's estimate of the chance of recovering revenue for a claim. Is it a 50 percent chance or a 20 percent chance of recovery? Risks are the project manager's estimate of things going wrong on the project due to subcontractors, liquidated damages, overhead expenses, and slower production. Not everything will go poorly, but some things will definitely end up costing the project more. I have used a risk/opportunity sheet to help ground executives in reality and not get too giddy about potential excess profits that may not materialize.

What are the earned values or quantity of work performed in the discrete activities you are tracking in your cost report? Are the quantities correct? Did you actually place 100 cubic yards of concrete in your foundation? Many field engineers like to adjust the quantities of work performed to match their costs. This, too, is wrong and only delays the reckoning of costs with revenue. I worked with one project manager who was extremely limber in his gymnastics of adjusting quantities performed to match costs. His executive was happy with his work until the end of the project when he discovered that the project had lost all its profit. I worked with another project manager who refused to be optimistic and didn't claim excess profit until he completed the project. His executive was frustrated with him during the project but very happy with him at the end. Proverbs 27:1 says, "Do not boast about tomorrow, for you do not know what a day may bring." Manage your revenue for today and be cautious about projecting revenue and profits before they are realized.

REPORTING ESTIMATED COST AT COMPLETION

As project manager, you are responsible for forecasting your ECAC. Beware of forecasting profit you will not realize. Proverbs 25:14 reminds us of the perils of disappointing results: "Like clouds and wind without rain is a man who boasts of a gift he does not give." I have been in many quarterly reviews with other project managers who got their butts chewed out because they missed their forecast of profit from

BEWARE OF FORECASTING PROFIT YOU WILL NOT REALIZE.

the previous quarter. How did they miss their forecast? Usually it's for one of three reasons:

1. Incompetence—They didn't know what to do.
2. Passive management—They knew what to do but didn't do it.
3. Actively hiding the ball—They intentionally and deceptively projected a greater profit.

How do you properly forecast your ECAC? A forecast is recognizing your costs-to-date with your quantities of production-to-date and estimating what costs remain to complete the work. For example, I might have a $40,000 budget to pour 100 feet of sidewalk 4 feet wide and 3.5 inches deep. After I complete 25 feet of sidewalk, my costs are $15,000 for purchase of the ready-mix concrete, labor, forms, and equipment to place the concrete. My unit cost would then be $600 per linear foot. If I have 75 feet left to complete, my estimated cost at completion is $600 multiplied by 75, which is $45,000; thus, my total cost for the activity is $60,000 ($15,000 plus $45,000) and is $20,000 over budget. This is known as the straight-line method of estimating cost at completion and is the simplest way to forecast costs at the end of the project. Most cost-accounting software will do this calculation for you in your cost report.

As project manager, you don't need to know every cost, detail, and projection. You can delegate the responsibility of cost management and forecasts to your discipline managers or engineers overseeing their piece of work. Beware of taking over their responsibility for managing their costs and projections. Keep them accountable with monthly reviews where they report on every line item in the cost report. During these meetings, you will see items that are going well and work that is going poorly. You can then discuss what to do about the work that is losing money and the causes of it. Do you have a greater quantity of work to do? If so, update your report so you can capture this overrun now. Determine the source of the quantity increase. Is it because of a change in field conditions, an increase in scope from your client, or just a bad estimate? Once you know the source, you can take action and submit a change request to your client or just work hard to make better production rates to reduce your losses. It is incredibly empowering to know where you are making money and where you are losing it. The unforgivable sin in project management is not knowing you are losing money until the end of the project.

On the other hand, a project manager can be too conservative in reserving profit and sandbag their projections by overestimating their remaining costs when they know many of them won't materialize. This can cause your executives to lose confidence in your projections and create tax problems regarding when the profit should be recognized. On one design-build project, I didn't recognize profit because we wanted to use the funds to further advance the design so we could later negotiate a large change order from the client. I then left the company for a better opportunity, and my successor immediately recognized a $2 million profit and appeared to be a star. I should have recognized the profit earlier and received the recognition and associated bonus for the project.

> **THE UNFORGIVABLE SIN IN PROJECT MANAGEMENT IS NOT KNOWING YOU ARE LOSING MONEY UNTIL THE END OF THE PROJECT.**

What are the best practices for reviewing your ECAC? In my field of work, our biggest cost is labor since we self-perform so much of the complex work. On one project, we had a weekly labor payroll of $1 million, which adds up very quickly. We were incurring so much cost in labor that we couldn't wait a month before reviewing, so we reviewed labor costs and projections on a weekly basis.

The next best practice is to do monthly reviews with your discipline managers, as we discussed above, and compare the ECAC budget against last month's ECAC. Reviewing the variance between these budgets will help you know when to revise your work plan to mitigate losses from poor production.

Another best practice is to conduct quarterly reviews with your key managers, controller, and executives. Usually executives, from their years of experience, can see through the fog of the project and intuitively know where you are doing well and where you are being too optimistic in improving your production rates. This quarterly meeting is a key accountability meeting to help project managers take the time to forecast their cost at completion. When it is not scheduled, many managers will just ignore the forecast because they are too busy building the project. So schedule these reviews to force yourself to be accountable while you still have time to jump sideways and complete your project with lower costs by working smarter.

Proverbs 10:9 instructs, "Whoever walks in integrity walks securely, but he who makes his ways crooked will be found out." If you hide costs and make rosy forecasts for profit, you will be found out. My deputy project manager always advocated the straight-line method for making projections. The cost accounting software allowed us to override those projections and put in a "Project Manager Goal," but my colleague always pushed to ignore that feature so we wouldn't end up lying to ourselves. I worked with another manager, however, who always knowingly overrode the straight-line projections to look good. He ended up being removed from the project because he never made his projections.

The ancients tell a captivating story of what happens when you grow lazy in your project management: "I passed by the field of a sluggard, by the vineyard of a man lacking sense, and behold, it was all overgrown with thorns; the ground was covered with nettles, and its stone wall was broken down. Then I saw and considered it; I looked and received instruction. A little sleep, a little slumber, a little folding of the hands to rest, and poverty will come upon you like a robber, and want like an armed man" (Proverbs 24:30–34). Be disciplined in reporting and estimating your cost at completion. Willfully ignoring costs because you don't want to see the results or passively ignoring them because you are too busy will reap the same results—poverty will come upon your project like a robber.

CASH FLOW

Cash is king! You can bankrupt your company or ruin year-end bonuses for all your employees and coworkers with a bad cash flow. I was on a tough project where our costs regularly exceeded our revenue, and every month was painful when we had to make cash calls to pay our bills. Because I was the reason for the cash calls, my executives never wanted to hear from me each month. So, be proactive in managing cash.

When you bid projects, you should do a cash flow study to obtain executive buyoff *before* starting the project. A key indicator in evaluating your performance is cash flow. This is because your company must plan to finance your project before your first invoice is paid by your client. This is true for internal projects, subcontracts, purchase orders, and any type of project. Projects always demand resources of personnel, engineering, shop drawings, equipment, materials, and perhaps insurance and bonds. Cash flow is key to staying in business and paying your bills.

When bidding a project, negotiate upfront terms with your client on large early purchases to assist your cash flow. If your project requires startup efforts of engineering, bonds, and insurance, put this cost into an early deliverable. This can range from 10 to 15 percent of your overall project costs. There is no reason for your company to carry this cost. Your work breakdown structure and your schedule should identify these deliverables and include budgets for them. These items then become part of your subcontract or purchase order. Do not finance your client's work. Get paid for your work up front!

Unfortunately, clients and prime contractors are usually late paying invoices. Your agreed terms may state payment is due within thirty or forty-five days of invoice, but you may not receive payment until after ninety days. What is your process when you're not paid? Who follows up with your clients on late payments? Whether your client is a public agency or a private company, they understand that you need to be paid for the project, but they are happy to delay payment and let you finance it.

Develop processes for your accounts receivable (AR) to be firm in collecting payments. Don't try to be a nice guy or overthink it. After sixty days have elapsed without receiving payment, your AR should automatically send a letter warning your client to pay within thirty days, or a lien will be filed on the project or company. Once that happens, it is amazing how quickly most clients will send a check. But if they don't, file a lien to protect your work. If they continue to delay payment, most contracts and subcontracts allow you to stop work until you get paid. Never apologize for collecting funds for the work you have performed. Be professional in administering your contract or purchase order, but always demand payment. You are not in the charity business. You work for profit.

When your projects are going poorly and you must make cash calls to your company or joint venture, it can be very emotional and trying. Every month, you must manage subcontractors and suppliers who are demanding payment and threatening to stop work. But you don't have the funds to pay them unless you get a fresh infusion of cash for your project. So do whatever is necessary to avoid finding yourself in this monthly stress of paying your bills while still trying to complete your project.

It is inevitable that you will sometimes have a problem project with poor cash flow. Recognize the issue early through good cost management and projections of cost at completion. Let your executives know in advance that you will need cash calls. I had one project where I knew we were in trouble, but I put off cash calls by revising my schedule of values with my client to get paid sooner. This helped for a while but made the future cash calls heavier. This also gave the executives a false sense of comfort that we were going to be okay—when I knew we had problems making our estimated cost at completion.

Learn from my mistakes. Keep your executives and managers informed of the problems early on so they are not surprised by the need to make cash calls. They can then put together a company-wide plan to manage these periods of low revenue.

Proverbs 6:6–8 contemplates an example from nature as inspiration for project management: "Go to the ant, O sluggard; consider her ways, and be wise. Without having any chief, officer, or ruler, she prepares her bread in summer and gathers her food in harvest." What are you doing to prepare for potential cash flow problems? Make a cash flow projection. Give your executives ample warning of problems. Then, hopefully, you can gather your food in harvest and be paid for the work you have performed on a timely basis.

CONCLUSION

Successful project management requires regular tracking of your production, costs, schedule, revenue, and forecasts of costs and associated profit at completion. What is tracked and monitored can be adjusted with timely changes to address costs and production. What is ignored will only get worse. Profit does not grow on trees; it only comes through good management and hard work. Order and cost savings never happen on their own. Track your performance early, and when you see trouble coming in delays and cost overruns, let your executives know so you can brainstorm together about how to better execute the project.

> **PROFIT DOES NOT GROW ON TREES; IT ONLY COMES THROUGH GOOD MANAGEMENT AND HARD WORK.**

KEY ACTION ITEMS

1. **Work Breakdown Structure (WBS)**—Delineate what detailed level of activities you want to roll up to your large headings or buckets of cost. Once you decide on these activities, set up cost codes and budgets for each one, then regularly review your costs. If your WBS is not sufficient to control your project, break it down into bite-sized pieces.

2. **Schedule**—Do not delegate your schedule to technicians. Be involved in setting up the schedule activities, logic ties, and sequence of work that defines your critical path. Understand and manage which activities can be completed concurrently and which are sequential. Review your monthly schedule updates to ensure they correctly define the critical path. Be careful not to create too many activities to track in your schedule.

3. **Costs**—Do not equate costs with revenue. Track your costs for the budgets you have set up for each item of work. Verify that your cost report is up to date with incurred costs (invoices, labor, supplies, etc.). Do not succumb to the temptation to manipulate your cost report to avoid reporting bad results.

4. **Revenue**—Revenue is the value of your executed contract or purchase order. It is what you are paid monthly for your project. Track revenue to ensure you have more money coming in than going out. Have a defined process in place for recognizing soft revenue from claims or client-promised change orders. (I only recognize revenue with an executed change order.) Keep a separate risk/opportunity sheet to track potential future revenue.

5. **Reporting Estimated Cost at Completion**—Review your cost report and ECAC. Use the straight-line method of forecasting cost at completion based on unit cost of production occurring to date. Hold your discipline managers accountable for preparing their portion of the forecasts. Do not be overly optimistic in forecasting

profit. Do not overpromise and underdeliver. Hold regular monthly and quarterly reviews.

6. **Cash Flow**—Cash is king! Be paid for the work you perform by setting up an accounts receivable process to send out notices and warnings of liens when not paid. Make a cash flow budget for your project before you start, and let executives know early if you need the company to finance your project with cash calls.

Part 2

VIBRANT PERSONAL LIFE

CHAPTER 8

BEWARE THE PITFALLS AND SNARES OF SUCCESS

For the simple are killed by their turning away, and the complacency of fools destroys them; but whoever listens to me will dwell secure and will be at ease, without dread of disaster.

PROVERBS 1:32–33

My friend Tim was well on his way to becoming incredibly successful. His business was thriving, and he had a great wife and two wonderful children. But then he had an affair. He lost his family and a significant part of his wealth through a divorce. How did this happen? My friend didn't just wake up one day and say, "Today I'm going to have an affair and cause incredible pain to those I've loved for twenty years." He started down the path to adultery by making several small, ill-advised decisions along the way. He became complacent and turned away from wisdom. As the opening verse warns: "The simple are killed by their turning away, and the complacency of fools destroys them" (Proverbs 1:32).

In Part 1 of this book, we explored the ancient wisdom needed to succeed in project management. In Part 2, we will uncover ancient truths to thrive in your personal life and avoid the traps and snares of success. We often try to compartmentalize our work life from our private life, but each bleeds into the other. You cannot thrive at work if your family life is in disarray; likewise, you cannot be what you should be to your family if your work life is blowing up and using up all your time and energy.

Unfortunately, Tim's story is not uncommon. We have all known colleagues whose choices ended up in disaster. So how do you avoid jeopardizing your career and family? In this chapter, we will identify the attitudes and actions that can lead you down the wrong path as you pursue a successful career. We will also explore how to develop a good defense and be alert to those temptations that can end up damaging your life.

THE SLIPPERY PATH

I don't know many highly successful managers and executives who have excelled in both their professional and personal lives. In fact, many in

> **ALL OF US CAN BE TEMPTED TO MAKE SMALL COMPROMISES ALONG THE PATH OF LIFE.**

my industry have failed relationships and broken families due to work demands and infidelity. All of us can be tempted to make small compromises along the path of life. Honestly, we often don't realize where the path of compromise is taking us until we end up doing things we never imagined. Proverbs 14:12 provides a warning that should shake us up and put us back on the right path: "There is a way that seems right to a man, but its end is the way to death." The slippery path starts with pride and self-deception and often ends in the death of our aspirations and the relationships we care most about.

Because of success and the confidence that comes from a full bank account and the praise of our peers, we may become proud and believe we are invulnerable and irreplaceable. Neither is true. Every successful person who has ever lived has been replaced by the next generation. We will all encounter health problems, relationship struggles, difficulties with our children, and challenges with our executives or boards. We are all vulnerable to failure and can be replaced, no matter how talented we are. Pride and self-deception lead us to an incorrect understanding of the precarious position we have in business and our families.

Pride also leads to a sense of entitlement. We may not want to admit this, but as we succeed, we become accustomed to being treated well, paid well, and given respect. We begin to think that this is who we are. We worked hard for our success. We deserve it, and now we should get a bigger piece of the pie. This entitled thinking is a trap that builds up our ego and subsequently leads to resentment and bitterness when we don't get what we think we deserve.

We can often recognize this pride or hubris in others. We see successful tech moguls or celebrities in the news spouting their opinions and expecting to be admired and listened to because they are famous or fabulously rich. But this pride that comes from success also applies to us. After several project wins, we may start thinking we know all the answers and stop listening and seeking advice. This pride is a trap that leads to unwise decisions. Proverbs 16:18 warns, "Pride goes before destruction, and a haughty spirit before a fall."

The slippery path begins with pride. Recognize that pride is not your friend. It can lead to foolish choices and a loss of reputation; therefore, erect boundaries to protect yourself from succumbing to pride.

> **WE MAY START THINKING WE KNOW ALL THE ANSWERS AND STOP LISTENING AND SEEKING ADVICE.**

DESTRUCTIVE SEXUAL RELATIONSHIPS

I took over managing a $500 million transit project in Los Angeles and hired a political consultant to help with the local jobs reporting.

This seasoned consultant told me to be careful working in Los Angeles. She had seen many successful men come to town and end up having affairs, ruining their marriages, and even losing their homes. I took her warning seriously and chose not to go out for drinks after work to avoid the danger of drinking when I was stressed, tired, and wanting friendly conversation.

Proverbs 5 provides a very detailed warning of what will happen if you enter into a reckless relationship: "Keep your way far from her, and do not go near the door of her house, lest you give your honor to others and your years to the merciless, lest strangers take their fill of your strength, and your labors go to the house of a foreigner, and at the end of your life you groan, when your flesh and body are consumed, and you say, 'How I hated discipline, and my heart despised reproof! I did not listen to the voice of my teachers or incline my ear to my instructors. I am at the brink of utter ruin in the assembled congregation'" (Proverbs 5:8–14). I quote this lengthy passage because it foretells what will happen if you give in to destructive sexual relationships: strangers will "take their fill of your strength, and your labors go to the house of a foreigner." In the end, you may be ruined financially, and all your hard work and success may go to others you do not know. This is exactly what my political consultant warned me about.

Sexual temptation has been around for thousands of years, and ancient wise men warned young men not to throw their lives away. "He who commits adultery lacks sense; he who does it destroys himself. He will get wounds and dishonor, and his disgrace will not be wiped away" (Proverbs 6:32–33). There are many powerful warnings in Proverbs: "Can one walk on hot coals and his feet not be scorched? So is he who goes in to his neighbor's wife; none who touches her will go unpunished" (Proverbs 6:28–29). No one wishes to destroy their life, but time after time, people succumb to this age-old temptation and pay the price. They may think they can afford to pay the price, but they don't realize how much it will cost them.

A seasoned entrepreneur shared at a workshop how he successfully grew his business and netted close to $100 million when he sold his company after twenty-five years. I and others in the meeting had the opportunity to ask him how he increased the value of his company and successfully sold it for such a high multiplier of his earnings before interest, taxes, and amortization (EBITA). As he shared his strategy of growing his employees and properly incentivizing them to align with the values of his company, he started talking about his one regret—an affair he'd had over twenty years prior. In tears, he admitted he was still paying the price for that bad decision, daily struggling to put his broken family back together. This is a man who had just sold his company with an incredible payday. But he still regretted that unwise decision that carried consequences he never imagined. King Solomon warns us about this remorse: "I find something more bitter than death: the woman whose heart is snares and nets, and whose hands are fetters. He who pleases God escapes her" (Ecclesiastes 7:26). This regret is not limited to men. Many successful women have had emotional affairs where they have given themselves to others.

You are now properly warned about this incredibly dangerous snare on the road to being a successful project manager. The way to avoid this trap is to first recognize you are susceptible to it. Traps and snares are hidden, or they wouldn't catch their prey. So beware; there are traps you cannot see. Next, set up good boundaries and a good defense. Professional football coaches say offense wins games; defense wins Super Bowls. Develop a good defense by not placing yourself in tempting situations. Practice the "Irish goodbye"—just walk away without saying goodbye. I have done this successfully multiple times. And plan ahead. Before Uber, I would always make sure I had my own rental car when traveling for business. That way, I could avoid ending up with drunk executives in a place I knew would lead to trouble.

SET UP GOOD BOUNDARIES AND A GOOD DEFENSE.

"With much seductive speech she persuades him; with her smooth talk she compels him. All at once he follows her, as an ox goes to the slaughter, or as a stag is caught fast till an arrow pierces its liver; as a bird rushes into a snare; he does not know that it will cost him his life" (Proverbs 7:21–23). Beware of this pitfall!

AVARICE

When my oldest son was five years old, he was adding up how much money he would have after his birthday. He exclaimed, "When Grandma gives me my birthday money, and I get money from my aunts and uncles, I'll have over $100!" My wife and I told him to quit being so greedy. Without missing a beat, he replied, "I'm not greedy; I just love money!" This story is cute when you are five years old, but chasing after wealth or material gain when you are an adult can control and ruin your life.

Proverbs 23:4–5 warns, "Do not toil to acquire wealth; be discerning enough to desist. When your eyes light on it, it is gone, for suddenly it sprouts wings, flying like an eagle toward heaven." Wealth is fleeting. Many successful people have gained a fortune and lost a fortune. Several of my colleagues lost millions of dollars in the dot-com bubble because they believed the bubble would never pop. (It took over fifteen years for the Nasdaq to recover.) Be careful not to exchange your life for riches that do not last.

> BE CAREFUL NOT TO EXCHANGE YOUR LIFE FOR RICHES THAT DO NOT LAST.

When you are greedy, you are not at peace with yourself or those around you. Proverbs 28:25 says, "A greedy man stirs up strife, but the one who trusts in the Lord will be enriched." Avarice (or greed) can actually stir up strife as you focus on gaining wealth.

Throughout the ages, people have often gained wealth by taking advantage of the poor and weak. Proverbs 22:16 warns, "Whoever oppresses the poor to increase his own wealth

. . . will only come to poverty." Some managers are tempted to take advantage of their employees and not pay them a fair wage. This is greed and will cause contention and problems as you incentivize people to do the bare minimum with low pay.

So, how do you avoid the pitfall of avarice? First, know that your security does not rest solely in riches. The Greek Stoic philosopher Epictetus wrote, "Wealth consists not in having great possessions, but in having few wants." As we will discuss in the next chapter, gratitude and generosity mark a successful life much more than a full bank account. Next, recognize that emotions are attached to investing and wealth. The main emotion that controls us is fear. Those of us who grew up in families with financial challenges may be afraid of losing our wealth, and as a result, we often toil to make sure we are putting enough money away for a rainy day. Our emotional view of scarcity controls us.

My son who loved money as a five-year-old is now, unsurprisingly, a financial planner. He regularly tells me that based on my investment portfolio, I only need to work if I want to, not because I have to. Sometimes I have a hard time heeding his advice because my fear of scarcity is still active. But I am slowly letting go of the need to accumulate. I control my wealth. It no longer controls me. I have finally concluded, as those who came before me, "Better is a little with the fear [reverent awe] of the Lord than great treasure and trouble with it" (Proverbs 15:16).

LYING AND FRAUD

The temptation to lie and commit small fraud is real. I took over a large project plagued with cost overruns. The cost report was a mess, and it took me a long time to find all the land mines the previous project manager had left. After six months, I thought I was done increasing the cost to completion. But then I found that the previous manager had overbooked revenue. He had written up all the time and material change orders and claimed the full amount of revenue, whether the work was completed or not. (This is claiming profit on work not performed.) I was angry, and I was tempted to hide what I had found because I was getting my butt kicked on the job. But I decided to be honest with my executives and give them the bad news that we had to reduce our recognized revenue. In the end, I was happy I came clean and didn't have to make up stories (lies) about lost revenue at the end of the project.

Lying and fraud are caused by greed and fear, and they have entrapped the most well-meaning project managers. You start out with little lies. You don't want to admit you are losing money on your project, so you intentionally lie on your reports by transferring costs to another cost code or inflating the quantities of your work performed. Once you start down the path of hiding your costs and increasing your revenue, you can't stop until you are found out. And rest assured, you will be discovered because you will eventually run out of funds and require cash infusions for your project. When this happens, Proverbs 1:19 will come true in your life: "Such are the ways of everyone who is greedy for unjust gain; it takes away the life of its possessors." Lying and fraud may not cause your death, but you may be fired or even end up in jail.

> **LYING AND FRAUD ARE CAUSED BY GREED AND FEAR, AND THEY HAVE ENTRAPPED THE MOST WELL-MEANING PROJECT MANAGERS.**

In the ancient world, fraud was often committed by intentionally deceiving others through physical signals (winks, pointing of fingers), similar to con artists and pickpockets today. Listen to how the ancients described a fraudulent person: "A worthless person, a wicked man, goes about with crooked speech, winks with his eyes, signals with his feet, points with his finger, with perverted heart devises evil, continually sowing discord; therefore calamity will come upon him suddenly; in a moment he will be broken beyond healing" (Proverbs 6:12–15). This is a harsh description, but accurate. Beware of fraud!

Besides lying about costs and revenue, don't fall into the trap of becoming a habitual liar who struggles with the truth. You may start fudging on the dates when the project will be completed and then blame the delay on somebody else. You may think you can protect your reputation by lying. But be warned, of the six things God hates, two of them have to do with lying: "The Lord hates . . . a lying tongue . . . a false witness who breathes out lies" (Proverbs 6:16–19). Why does God despise lying? It is because it is so damaging to yourself and others. When you lie, you end up deceiving yourself and destroying your reputation. You also harm others by giving a false testimony of their acts. Many people's reputations and careers have been hurt by false accusations.

Several times I have been put in an awkward position when my executives lied about my project to try to delay having to give an account. Inevitably, higher-level executives would then ask for a detailed account of the financials. What did I do? Fortunately, I was always honest with my joint venture, and I would simply provide the documentation of the issues I had already shared at the project level. Proverbs 10:9 states, "Whoever walks in integrity walks securely, but he who makes his ways crooked will be found out." I have consciously protected my reputation by not falling into the strong temptation to lie just a little. Remember, "A good name is to be chosen rather than great riches" (Proverbs 22:1).

Don't fall into the trap of lying and fraud. They only buy you a little time, and they can cost you your job, employment, and family. If you don't believe me, talk to the executives at Enron who went to jail for fraud.

SELF-MEDICATION AND ADDICTIONS

Many successful people struggle with addiction. I know several child-hood friends who became addicted to drugs and alcohol and died in their fifties.

It is very sad to see good people unexpectedly die due to the det-rimental health effects of addiction. One of my colleagues didn't show up at work for several days, and no one could reach him. We finally had the police check on him, and they found him dead in his apartment. None of us knew he had been drinking for two weeks straight and not eating. At fifty-three years old, his body gave out, and he died completely alone. So, as you deal with the stress and demands of life, beware of the temptation to self-medicate with alcohol and drugs. As the ancients warn, "Do not look at wine when it is red, when it sparkles in the cup and goes down smoothly. In the end it bites like a serpent and stings like an adder" (Proverbs 23:31–32).

I was surprised to read an article in *Fortune* about tech executives in Silicon Valley who are "reportedly taking ketamine and attending psychedelic parties to bolster their focus and creativity."[14] These tech moguls are under tremendous pressure to invent, discover, or develop the next big thing, and they often look to drugs to help them get an edge on their competition. But even if this works for a time, it is only a short-term solution. Studies have shown that hallucinogens (LSD, marijuana, mushrooms, etc.) can have long-term detrimental effects on mental health, including dissociation, sedation, anxiety, and even schizophrenia. Crystal meth (speed) can also cause schizophrenia. Drugs and alcohol are not the answer to the challenges of life.

In fact, drugs and alcohol more often increase your problems. Proverbs 20:1 says, "Wine is a mocker, strong drink a brawler, and whoever is led astray by it is not wise." Drug use and excessive drinking make it difficult to control your temper and make healthy emotional choices. They are extremely destructive to your family and often cause long-term psychological problems in your spouse and children.

I have a brother who struggled with drug addiction for twenty years. Our prayers were finally answered when he was arrested and sent to jail for six months. Being in jail and experiencing terrible daily pain from withdrawal and rotting teeth made him come to grips with his bad decisions. In those moments of sobriety, he gave his life to God, which provided the strength he needed to stay off drugs. When he got out of jail, he reengaged with his family and regularly attended church and Narcotics Anonymous for support and accountability. His felony was eventually expunged, and he had a successful career as a safety professional in construction. Ironically, his background helped him recognize workers under the influence of alcohol or drugs, so he was able to remove them from the job for their own safety. Be encouraged. There is a way out of drugs and alcohol if you seek help.

Besides being aware of this snare, how do you avoid becoming addicted to alcohol or drugs? First, know that drugs and alcohol only provide temporary relief and do not solve your problems. Next, have the courage to identify the core problems driving you to self-medicate. What pain, fear, or insecurity are you trying to run from or cover up? Then, talk to a trusted friend or counselor to help identify and work through these problems.

ANGER, BITTERNESS, AND ENVY

Anger and outrage seem to be everywhere—in the news, on social media, and on college campuses. Many people think they have the right to emotionally vomit on others when they feel offended or believe that they have somehow been wronged. Just imagine the damage done when successful project managers exhibit this type of temper-tantrum behavior. We are admonished by the wise to "Make no friendship with a man given to anger, nor go with a wrathful man, lest you learn his

> **ANGER IS A SELF-LAID SNARE THAT WILL ENTRAP YOU.**

ways and entangle yourself in a snare" (Proverbs 22:24–25). Anger is a self-laid snare that will entrap you.

One construction manager I worked with was incredibly talented at cursing and making the veins pop out on his neck and face when he was angry. I would watch in awe as he yelled at me, thinking, *I could never curse this fluently or make my face turn that red even if I took a six-week course on how to be angry.* I would then calmly answer his questions and walk away, which made him angrier. This man's anger limited his career advancement.

Proverbs 25:28 gives a great visual picture of someone who cannot control their anger: "A man without self-control is like a city broken into and left without walls." In the ancient world, a city's walls protected them from attack. Now imagine an abundantly rich city without any walls, open for bandits to come and go as they pleased, robbing and killing the inhabitants. This is what an angry person is. They have no defenses and are open to being taken advantage of because all that controls them is their rage.

"Be angry and do not sin; do not let the sun go down on your anger, and give no opportunity to the devil" (Ephesians 4:26–27). It is not always sinful or wrong to be angry. Unjust and cruel actions by others may demand an angry response. But we are not to let anger take over our lives. The idea of not letting the sun go down on your anger means to keep short accounts and deal with the anger the day it occurs. Do not let it fester and grow into bitterness that can take hold of you and poison all your achievements and relationships. A few verses later, the Apostle Paul writes, "Let all bitterness and wrath and anger and clamor and slander be put away from you, along with all malice" (Ephesians 4:31). This advice is good for our mental and emotional health.

Bitterness is dangerous and difficult to get rid of. When I was young, a wise woman told me bitterness is like making poison to give to the person with whom you are angry but drinking it yourself. Guard your heart that you "do not rejoice when your enemy falls, and let not your heart be glad when he stumbles" (Proverbs 24:17). If you find yourself wishing ill for others, hoping they will fail, you have become bitter. Another ancient writer warns, "See to it that no . . . 'root of bitterness' springs up and causes trouble, and by it many become defiled" (Hebrews 12:15). Bitterness doesn't just affect you; it poisons or defiles those around you.

I have experienced several professional and personal betrayals in my career. These betrayals made me angry, and I struggled not to become bitter and wish ill on those who wronged me. For years I waited to experience "what goes around comes around." I wanted payback, but I wasn't in a position to give it. Because of the betrayals, I moved on from the companies I had worked for and the projects into which I had poured my life and blood. After a few years, I could see that I was in a better place, working for a better company and sharing in the profits. This helped minimize the pain of betrayal, but I still wanted retribution. The only way I got over this was to forgive the people who had caused me harm. I did this not for them (they never asked); I did this for myself, to stop the root of bitterness from growing in me.

Right behind anger and bitterness is the destructive trap of envy. Envy is a "painful or resentful awareness of an advantage enjoyed by another joined with a desire to possess the same advantage."[15] Envy is seeing others who are clearly not as deserving as you receive the recognition and promotion you believe you deserve. No matter what level you reach in an organization, you will still encounter the temptation of envy. Proverbs 14:30 explains what envy does: "A tranquil heart gives life to the flesh, but envy makes the bones rot." Envy eats away at you. It makes you discontented down to the very structural foundation of your body.

Even though I have sought to live a balanced life of wisdom, I am regularly susceptible to envy. When on social media I see the great experiences people are having and their fabulously talented, successful children, I'm tempted to compare lives and want theirs. Have you experienced that? We measure ourselves and our lives against others and feel we come up short. All of us are tempted to think that life is greener elsewhere.

Early in my career, I worked for a design firm and saw many engineers around me being promoted to associates of the company. Once an associate, you could start sharing in the profits of the company. I, of course, compared myself to those being promoted, and I didn't see them as any better than myself. I had passed my professional engineer's exam, I was converted to salary, and I was billable at seventy hours per week, but still no promotion. I was envious and irritated, but I kept my head down and didn't let up on the quality or production of my design work. Not long after, one of the firm's clients asked me to become a construction design manager for them. They were a major contractor, and this was a great opportunity. When I told the senior vice president at the design firm about the offer, I asked what incentive there was to stay if they weren't going to promote me to associate. He told me there were no promises, but to just keep working. I moved on and never looked back.

The psalmist writes, "Fret not yourself because of evildoers; be not envious of wrongdoers! For they will soon fade like the grass and wither like the green herb" (Psalm 37:1–2). I can't say that my bosses who didn't promote me were *evildoers*, but I felt it was definitely wrong. To not fret is to be content with the life you have and leave the things you cannot control to God. He will bring about justice.

How do you avoid the pitfalls of anger, bitterness, and envy? There is no easy, quick fix, but it starts with taking responsibility for how you're feeling. I suggest doing a self-imposed audit of your emotional and spiritual health. You may not have the perspective to do this on your own, so ask your spouse and/or good friends for feedback in your life. Ask if they think you are an angry person. If they see you as content or dissatisfied. Ask if they like being around you and why. You may be surprised by what you hear.

Take the time to do regular check-ins on yourself. It's for your own good, the good of your family, and those you work with. Don't let your life be poisoned by anger, bitterness, and envy.

In the next chapter, we will discuss positive steps you can take to care for yourself and build boundaries and habits that lead to long-term personal and professional success.

CONCLUSION

Discussing the pitfalls and snares of successful project managers is disconcerting. It can produce fear that you have the potential to blow out your life. But some fear can be healthy and protect you from taking stupid risks, similar to signs near the top of a cliff that warn you to stay away from the edge. You may not know the cliff is eroding and could crumble beneath you. That is my purpose for writing this chapter—to help make you aware of the traps and snares that can entangle you and bring about disaster. Proverbs warns us of the consequences of not heeding correction: "He who is often reproved, yet stiffens his neck, will suddenly be broken beyond healing" (Proverbs 29:1).

Once you identify the dangers you face as a successful manager, you can put into place a plan and barriers to keep you away from the crumbling cliff that could harm your life. But you must take the warnings seriously. They don't just apply to others; they apply to you. You are just as susceptible as those in multiple generations before you who have fallen. One of the humbling admonitions I keep at the forefront of my mind is, "So let the man who feels sure of his standing today be careful that he does not fall tomorrow" (1 Corinthians 10:12, JBP).

KEY ACTION ITEMS

1. **The Slippery Path**—Pride is the lubricant on the path that leads to slipping and falling. Guard yourself from believing you are invulnerable and will never fail, or you can become entitled and think you deserve more for your work and leadership. Beware of the trap

of pride and ego. Make sure you have people in your life who keep you accountable and give you honest feedback (friends, not fans).

2. **Destructive Sexual Relationships**—Many stronger and better people have fallen into this snare and destroyed their lives. Realize the great costs and consequences reckless sexual relationships will have on your family and reputation. Know that you are susceptible to this trap, and develop a good defense to avoid it. Do not place yourself alone, with alcohol and weariness, in a potentially dangerous situation. Practice the "Irish goodbye" and just walk away.

3. **Avarice**—Don't let greed and the pursuit of wealth steal your life. Wealth is fleeting. We all know people who have lost money, but we don't think it will apply to us. Realize that fear of scarcity may drive your decisions. Choose to live below your means, be content, and invest relationally in your family, who will carry on your legacy after you are gone.

4. **Lying and Fraud**—Fear and greed lead to lying and fraud. Beware that this begins with small lies and fudges that can develop into fraud that could put you in jail. Don't start down the path of willfully adjusting your financial reporting. There is no better defense than the truth. When there are financial problems, come clean right away and then try to recover the losses.

5. **Self-Medication and Addictions**—Beware of self-medicating your pain and stress with alcohol and drugs. This only provides temporary relief and can lead to an early death. Depressants (alcohol), hallucinogens (LSD, marijuana), and stimulants (crystal meth) all cause massive health problems and can lead to long-term mental health issues. Recognize the symptoms of addiction early and get help through counseling and a twelve-step program.

6. **Anger, Bitterness, and Envy**—Don't be discontented and poison yourself with anger, bitterness, and envy. Do regular emotional check-ins on yourself. Ask your spouse and/or good friends for feedback. Take responsibility for your emotional health.

CHAPTER 9
CREATE LONG-TERM SUCCESS

Riches and honor are with me, enduring wealth and righteousness. My fruit is better than gold, even fine gold, and my yield than choice silver. I walk in the way of righteousness, in the paths of justice, granting an inheritance to those who love me, and filling their treasuries.

PROVERBS 8:18–21

When I was twenty-six, I was dating a beautiful woman way above my class and trying to decide if I should ask her to marry me. I had heard some long-married couples confess that at least once in their lives they had questioned whether they married the right person. I didn't want to have regrets. I wanted my decision to be sound and not based solely on love and desire. So I did what engineers do: I made a matrix of the pros and cons to marrying this amazing woman. I analyzed my list, prayed about it, and then realized I was being an idiot. It all came down to one simple question: "Could I imagine life without her?" The answer was a resounding, "No." So I proposed, and we've been happily married for over thirty years.

Marrying my wife is the absolute best decision I have ever made. Through this and many other wise choices in my life, I have seen firsthand that the fruit of wisdom is "better than gold, even fine gold, and my yield than choice silver" (Proverbs 8:19).

When we are young, as I was at twenty-six, we often don't realize the consequences our choices and habits will have on the rest of our lives. Developing good habits and making wise decisions is like compounding interest, the eighth wonder of the world, where our initial investment grows beyond what we can imagine. When we make wise decisions, the rewards we reap greatly exceed the initial value of the choice we made at a certain point in time.

This chapter will explore the wisdom and practices needed to *thrive* in your personal life. Beyond recognizing and avoiding snares that can hinder and even ruin your life (as explored in the last chapter), you can move forward confidently and live meaningfully by practicing humility, prioritizing a good marriage, pursuing abundance and generosity, developing contentment, accepting correction, and cultivating hope and joy.

PRACTICE HUMILITY

Knowledge and technology are always progressing. They are not static facts like the elevation of Mount Kilimanjaro (19,341 feet). Even the details and rhythms of our daily lives seem to fluctuate. So, it is important to stay humble and hungry to learn so you can adapt to these changes and continue to succeed. The pathway to success and refreshment is to "be not wise in your own eyes; fear the Lord and turn away from evil. It will be healing to your flesh and refreshment to your bones" (Proverbs 3:7–8). Long-term satisfaction comes through humility.

> **LONG-TERM SATISFACTION COMES THROUGH HUMILITY.**

For the past thirty years, I have worked with a fabulous quality engineer. When I first met Piyush, he worked in the field while I was in the office, so I didn't have the opportunity to fully appreciate his competence and diligence. He excelled on that project, but he rarely received any recognition. When he left to be a quality engineer on a project in another state, his boss took credit for his work. A few years later, we had the chance to work together again on a bus rapid transit project. Once again, he excelled, and people finally began to notice. Piyush didn't demand recognition; he just humbly kept working and made money on everything he touched. I had the privilege of working with him on my last large project, and he became my most trusted ally in overcoming preferential comments from the owner's representatives. Piyush is the only person I know who has always been technically correct. How does he accomplish this? Through humility. He is a lifelong learner who never stops acquiring knowledge. I now can confidently say that he has forgotten more about concrete than I ever knew. What a privilege to work daily with someone who makes you a better project manager because their humble diligence pushes you also to be excellent.

How do you keep learning when you think you already know everything about your industry? Remaining humble keeps you hungry to learn, and it is the cure for pride. So, how do you stay humble when you have achieved success? You must recognize that your success is not just because of you. Others have invested in your life and mentored and guided you. Your family, friends, and coworkers have helped you gain emotional intelligence and provided perspective and wisdom. You have good team members who contributed to the success of the project.

Proverbs 27:2 states, "Let another praise you, and not your own mouth; a stranger, and not your own lips." I recently obtained a major victory in closing out a project. I can't praise myself for this accomplishment because it wasn't all me. Yes, I led the team and helped others smarter than I perform at a high level. My leadership contributed to the victory. But to stay humble, I thank my team for their good work, and we celebrate together. Any time I receive a compliment from a client or executive, I always point to those on my team who worked behind the scenes to make the project a success. This isn't being falsely modest; it is the truth.

The essence of humility is having the right opinion of yourself—not too high and not too low. You know you have strengths in your

> **THE ESSENCE OF HUMILITY IS HAVING THE RIGHT OPINION OF YOURSELF—NOT TOO HIGH AND NOT TOO LOW.**

technical knowledge and leadership skills, but you also know you can improve and learn from others. That is humility, and it starts with recognizing that all that is good comes from God. The psalmist declares, "Oh, how abundant is your goodness, which you have stored up for those who fear you and worked for those who take refuge in you" (Psalm 31:19).

Several years ago, I visited Churchill Downs, the famous racetrack of the Kentucky Derby. Before the race, I visited the horses in their stables and picked my winners based on how the horses looked. I didn't place any bets, but I was curious to see how I would fare if I had. Unsurprisingly, all my picks lost.

Humility is realizing you can be wrong and that you need to slow down and consider the right path to take. If you move forward without thinking through your decisions or getting counsel, it is like picking horses to win a race—most of your choices will be wrong.

Pursue humility throughout your life. It will protect you from believing your own press and keep you from becoming entitled and making stupid mistakes. Seek to be humble, not to be admired but because you know it is the right way to live and comes with untold rewards. "The reward for humility and fear of the Lord is riches and honor and life" (Proverbs 22:4).

PRIORITIZE A GOOD MARRIAGE

I distinctly remember three times in my professional career when I was extremely discouraged (probably depressed) because of professional betrayal by what I thought were my friends and colleagues. As a result, I had to leave these organizations and move on. My wife literally saved me during these times by comforting me and validating my feelings. If she could have, she would have tackled those executives and scratched their eyes out for how they treated me. It was invaluable to know I had somebody in my corner who believed in me and kindly encouraged me to keep going. She had faith in me when I had no faith in myself. It is wonderful to be known and loved at your weakest times in life. She didn't love me for performing at a high level. She loved me for who I was with all the trappings of success stripped away.

Good marriages are a treasure for life. They are a source of joy, strength, confidence, encouragement, and companionship. I cannot overemphasize how much a good marriage contributes to long-term success in business and thriving in your personal life.

If you are struggling in your marriage, don't give up. Cultivating a good marriage is worth the effort. Below are some marriage-strengthening practices my wife and I have implemented over the years to create a nurturing, loving relationship.

See Your Spouse as a Gift from God—Proverbs 19:14 says, "House and wealth are inherited from fathers, but a prudent wife is from the Lord." I told my wife when we got married that she would always be a reminder of God's grace in my life. Grace is receiving a gift that is not earned. My wife is a gift from God I do not deserve. Her presence in my life reminds me of God's goodness. "He who finds a wife finds a good thing and obtains favor from the Lord" (Proverbs 18:22).

But realistically, we understand that our spouse can also be a source of irritation and frustration. This is not a new challenge; it has been around for thousands of years. Proverbs 21:9 states, "It is better to live in a corner of the housetop than in a house shared with a quarrelsome wife." It is not just wives that can be contentious. Men can be cruel, offensive, and just as difficult to live with. Maybe this is why many men hang out in their garages and women in their she sheds.

Often, we give our spouse reason to be contentious and, once the offensive pattern starts, it is difficult to stop. Proverbs 27:15-16 paints this picture as a warning; "A continual dripping on a rainy day and a quarrelsome wife are alike; to restrain her is to restrain the wind or to grasp oil in one's right hand." My colleague, Jim, would spend long hours at work and then hang out with his work friends on the weekends. One Saturday morning, he didn't show up for the scheduled bike ride. Come Monday, we asked what had happened, and he replied, "Well, I was going out the door and then the talking started." We all laughed, having experienced "the talking" ourselves. We also knew that we often deserved the talking because we hadn't prioritized or valued our spouses and families the way we should have.

Despite occasional irritations, you can choose to focus on what you appreciate about your spouse instead of what frustrates you. You did little to nothing to deserve the gift of your spouse loving you and sharing their life with you. So, say thank you often. Choosing gratitude is an important step toward creating a healthy marriage. Proverbs 31:10 comments on the incredible value of a good marriage partner: "An excellent wife who can find? She is far more precious than jewels."

There is a story of a man from the Pacific Islands who negotiated a dowry for his wife. In his culture, the common dowry price for a wife was three to five cows. This man, in negotiating with his bride's father, offered the outrageous dowry of *eight* cows for a woman who the villagers thought of as plain—homely. The whole village was stunned, never imagining this woman was worth eight cows. They concluded that the father must have greatly out negotiated the groom. The man married his bride and took her back to his village on another island. Six months later, several villagers visited the newlyweds and were amazed at the bride's transformation into a beautiful, gracious, and loving wife. They asked what happened, and her husband replied, "She is an eight-cow bride, and I treat her like a treasure." When you are thankful and communicate what a wonderful gift your spouse is, they begin to act like the gift they are.

Build a Good Offense—In the previous chapter, we discussed how to develop a good defense to avoid infidelity. A good offense is to enjoy the spouse God has given you. Proverbs 5:15–19 wisely informs us where we should meet our sexual needs: "Drink water from your own cistern, flowing water from your own well. Should your springs be scattered abroad, streams of water in the streets? Let them be for yourself alone, and not for strangers with you. Let your fountain be blessed, and rejoice in the wife of your youth, a lovely deer, a graceful doe. Let her breasts fill you at all times with delight; be intoxicated always in her love." I quote the whole passage here so you can see how explicit the instruction is. Water is a metaphor for sexual relations. We are only to drink water from our own cistern—that is, from our own spouse.

The reason I titled this section a "Good Offense" is that one of the best ways to avoid infidelity is to proactively seek satisfaction in your marriage. When you delight in your spouse, you don't have eyes for others. Thriving in life is enjoying sexual relations in the safety of marriage.

You can't have a good offense without a game plan. It doesn't just happen on its own. Men and women are sexually aroused differently. Most men are like a light bulb—just flip the switch and they're ready to go. Most women are more like a clothes iron. It takes a while for them to warm up. Men are visually stimulated. Women are usually more relationally stimulated. They often want to connect emotionally before connecting physically. These stereotypes are not always the case and may be reversed. There are times my wife is aroused, but I need to first connect with her emotionally because I'm irritated by something she said earlier in the day.

> **WHEN YOU DELIGHT IN YOUR SPOUSE, YOU DON'T HAVE EYES FOR OTHERS.**

These differences highlight the need to have a game plan that works for your marriage. For example, arrange your schedules to go to bed together. There is no better sex advice than to "Go to bed together!" This allows time to connect at the end of a busy day, talk about the kids, and share your struggles. My wife and I try to pray together every night before we go to sleep. Sometimes I fall asleep while praying, and she shakes me to keep me awake, but this practice has been great for our peace of mind and relationship.

One of the biggest obstacles to "drinking from your own cistern" is to have a television in the bedroom and watch news, sports, or just stupid shows before bed. This mindless distraction steals your life, most likely irritates your spouse, and often causes anxiety. Get the television out of the room. Keep your bedroom free from clutter and instead create a romantic atmosphere. (If you don't know how to do this, delegate it to your spouse—you will be pleasantly surprised.)

Finally, a good offense is to plan time together weekly, monthly, and yearly. Most spouses spell love as T-I-M-E. If you want to demonstrate your love to your spouse, be intentional and plan date nights and getaways together. When we had young kids, the best thing my wife and I did for our marriage was to go away overnight every year to connect and refresh.

My son got married in the summer of 2020, and my wife and I hosted the wedding reception in our backyard because no indoor parties were allowed due to COVID. When it was my turn to toast my son and his bride, I was overwhelmed at the good gift God had chosen for my son in his amazing wife. As a parent, it is difficult to trust others to provide for our children. But the Lord gave my child a gift much greater than I could have ever picked out.

Enjoy and celebrate your spouse. It is foundational to a meaningful and successful life.

PURSUE ABUNDANCE AND GENEROSITY

Living a life of generosity is a key ingredient to thriving in life and is the antidote for greed. Generosity changes your perspective from grasping to blessing. Many of us live with a scarcity mindset, believing that there are only so many pieces of pie to go around. If I give somebody a piece of my pie, then there is less pie left for me. This perspective leads to greed, pessimism, and selfishness. To thrive, we need to nurture an attitude of gratitude, recognize the blessings and abundance we have and, in response, live a life of generosity. When we are generous, we are surprised by the returns of a richer, fuller life.

In 1992, my wife and I visited Croatia during the Yugoslav Wars to serve displaced refugees. While we were there, we connected with Irena, our bright eighteen-year-old Croatian translator who spoke wonderful English. We asked Irena what she wanted to do with her life, and she expressed a deep desire to study English Literature and the Bible. Because of the war and her status as a refugee, however, her options for higher education were limited. We had just bought a house near Biola, a Christian liberal arts university that offered leadership scholarships to gifted foreign students. We suggested she apply and promised that if she were accepted, she could live with us for at least the first year. Six months after returning from our trip, we received a phone call from Irena. She was coming to America! This started a beautiful, abundant relationship in which we received far more than we ever gave. Now, every two to four years, we return to Croatia for incredible vacations in villas on the Adriatic with Irena and her whole extended family.

"One gives freely, yet grows all the richer; another withholds what he should give, and only suffers want. Whoever brings blessing will be enriched, and one who waters will himself be watered" (Proverbs 11:24–25). As my wife and I discovered with Irena, generosity turns out to be reciprocal. If you want to grow your wealth, give freely. I don't know why or how this works, but it is true. When you hold all your resources in an open hand and give to those in need, you receive back more than you gave.

> **IF YOU WANT TO GROW YOUR WEALTH, GIVE FREELY.**

Proverbs 21:13 says, "Whoever closes his ear to the cry of the poor will himself call out and not be answered." This verse always convicts me. As a best practice, I regularly give to rescue missions in the locations of my projects. I often see the homeless and poor on my way to and from work, so I give to the organizations that strive to bring long-term solutions to the area.

My brother worked nights as a safety manager on a transit project in south central Los Angeles, and he always carried care packages in his truck to give to those in need. The homeless appreciated his generosity —cans of soup, bottles of water, and granola bars—and then wouldn't vandalize the project. Proverbs 19:17 says, "Whoever is generous to the poor lends to the Lord, and he will repay him for his deed."

Irena taught my wife and me a simple but profound saying: "Slow and steady." Through war and other trials, she learned the importance of persevering through tough times and continuing to make wise choices. This adage is also true for gaining wealth. Proverbs 13:11 tells us, "Wealth gained hastily will dwindle, but whoever gathers little by little will increase it."

There is no fast track to riches. Most millionaires in the United States are those who have lived below their means and regularly contributed to their retirement plans. In project management, it is best to turn a profit little by little through good cost management. If you make a windfall without good systems, you will become overconfident and have losses on future projects. Slow and steady is the way to go.

Proverbs 28:19 says, "Whoever works his land will have plenty of bread, but he who follows worthless pursuits will have plenty of poverty." Every year or so, I am contacted by salesmen who tell me how great my return on investment will be for whatever they're promoting, and I'm tempted to roll the dice. But if it sounds too good to be true, it probably is. I admit that I got greedy and chased the dot-com growth market in 2001. I saw how big the returns were and jumped on the bandwagon only to lose thousands of dollars.

When we are greedy or grasping, we are controlled by fear of missing out and not by the perspective of blessing others with the abundance we already have. Generosity is the key to long-term financial success and a full life.

DEVELOP CONTENTMENT

Great peace comes from being content in all circumstances. This is easy to say but difficult to achieve.

The Apostle Paul, who lived an exceptionally hard but deeply impactful life, wrote, "I have learned, in whatever situation I am, to be content. I know how to be brought low, and I know how to abound. In any and every circumstance, I have learned the secret of facing plenty and hunger, abundance and need. I can do all things through him who strengthens me" (Philippians 4:11–13). Paul's secret was dependence on God for all good things.

Contentment is being satisfied with having your basic needs met. My dad grew up in the 1930s during the Great Depression. When I was a child and would ask for some new toy, he would say, "Boy, what more do you need? You have food on your plate, a roof over your head, and socks on your feet!" My dad knew how to be content.

Ancient wisdom affirms this: "Remove far from me falsehood and lying; give me neither poverty nor riches; feed me with the food that is needful for me, lest I be full and deny you and say, 'Who is the Lord?' or lest I be poor and steal and profane the name of my God" (Proverbs 30:8–9).

Contentment doesn't come from how much we have but from a life well lived—in our work and relationships. Proverbs 12:14 says, "From the fruit of his mouth a man is satisfied with good, and the work of a man's hand comes back to him." Notice that enjoying the work of our hands is also tied to the fruit of our mouth. The work we do and the words we speak can bring anger and anxiety or peace and contentment.

A true sign of contentment is showing kindness to others, not for personal gain, but because we have the capacity and confidence to be a blessing to others. Proverbs 21:21 says, "Whoever pursues righteousness

KINDNESS IS LIVING WITH OPEN HANDS.

and kindness will find life, righteousness, and honor." Kindness is living with open hands, acknowledging that we are simply stewards of what has been given to us. When we act with kindness and gratitude, we find life and honor. We also find contentment.

ACCEPT CORRECTION

Often, the path to thriving in life requires making course corrections along the way. There are times we don't realize we're off course, and we need someone to speak truth to us and, if necessary, challenge us to correct our behavior. Proverbs 17:10 says, "A rebuke goes deeper into a man of understanding than a hundred blows into a fool." Many of us choose to be around only those who like us and compliment our work, but to succeed in life, we must stay open to correction and welcome those who will call us to account.

It is never pleasant to be rebuked or corrected. Hebrews 12:11 says, "For the moment all discipline seems painful rather than pleasant, but later it yields the peaceful fruit of righteousness to those who have been trained by it." Notice the result of discipline is the "peaceful fruit of righteousness." Constructive discipline *improves* us, but it should be motivated by love and concern. "My son, do not despise the Lord's discipline or be weary of his reproof, for the Lord reproves him whom he loves, as a father the son in whom he delights" (Proverbs 3:11–12). The opposite of love is apathy. So, if a friend, family member, or colleague doesn't warn you about your unwise or bad behavior, they don't truly care about you.

I encourage you to be open to correction and actively seek it. Build a close-knit team of colleagues and friends who promise to speak to you honestly about your life. Proverbs 12:1 says, "Whoever loves discipline loves knowledge, but he who hates reproof is stupid." We can only thrive in our lives when others point out our blind spots and help correct our self-deceptions. We all need honest feedback and, at times, correction. Be willing to learn and adjust course.

CULTIVATE HOPE AND JOY

The "pursuit of happiness" is one of the unalienable rights listed in America's Declaration of Independence. Intrinsic to who we are is the desire for this happiness or joy, but how can we attain it?

Joy is the fruit of hope and a life well lived. I recently had a radical prostatectomy and found myself depressed two months after surgery. As I was recovering and dealing with the effects of the surgery, I lost hope for the future. I cognitively knew many people had much worse health problems than I, but I still lost hope. Proverbs 13:12 was coming true in my life: "Hope deferred makes the heart sick, but a desire fulfilled is a tree of life." So how was I to restore hope?

JOY IS THE FRUIT OF HOPE AND A LIFE WELL LIVED.

I needed to take my eyes off my circumstances and start looking outward. The surgery was successful, and I was cancer-free, but I was still listless. I told my leadership coach that I used to be able to push through issues even at 60 percent strength. Now, weeks after my surgery, I couldn't exercise without needing a nap, and I could only work maybe four hours a day. No longer could I just grunt through it and move forward. I was discouraged! I needed a change of heart to start looking forward with hope. And I couldn't do this on my own, which added to the depression. Proverbs 18:14 concisely states what I was experiencing: "A man's spirit will endure sickness, but a crushed spirit who can bear?"

Looking forward is a different emotional mindset than just moving forward out of obligation and responsibility. Looking forward involves hope. At the urging of my wife, I started planning things that would restore my strength: I signed up for golf lessons, hired a personal trainer, and started scheduling bi-weekly massages. (In the past, such indulgences would have been unthinkable.) I also made sure I engaged my mind and socialized. Even though I was still physically struggling, I started going to my client's office twice a week for a half day to be mentally stimulated. During all of this, I continued the good habits I had earlier developed of daily Bible reading, going to bed with my wife, sleeping seven to eight hours a night, and eating healthy meals.

The problem with depression is stated in Proverbs 14:10: "The heart knows its own bitterness, and no stranger shares its joy." You feel alone in your depression, and you are often ashamed to admit you are struggling.

If you're suffering from depression, I encourage you to get help and not isolate yourself in a dark place. Fortunately, my wife was my advocate and helped me walk out of this low patch. I never doubted God's goodness, but I had emotionally lost hope and an optimistic view of the future.

Hope is essential to a life of joy. Proverbs 15:13 says, "A glad heart makes a cheerful face, but by sorrow of heart the spirit is crushed."

The wise ancients often wrote about joy: "A joyful heart is good medicine, but a crushed spirit dries up the bones" (Proverbs 17:22).

"The cheerful of heart has a continual feast" (Proverbs 15:15).

"The hope of the righteous brings joy" (Proverbs 10:28).

I quote all these verses to show that the wise teachers of the past thought about and obtained joy. A joyful life is possible!

Nehemiah, who in 445 BC oversaw rebuilding the walls around Jerusalem after they had been destroyed by the Babylonians, wrote, "The joy of the Lord is your strength" (Nehemiah 8:10). Nehemiah had lived as a captive in Babylon and could have been a very angry, bitter, and depressed person. But he admonished the Israelites to find strength in the Lord's joy. This is a life-changing truth. We are not alone, and we do not have to depend upon our own strength for joy. Our strength to persevere through difficult circumstances and the trials of life comes from the joy of the Lord.

The Apostle Paul makes a similar admonishment: "Rejoice in the Lord always; again I will say, rejoice" (Philippians 4:4). We are to *choose* to rejoice in God. We have the choice, the agency, and, therefore, the ability to choose joy.

Obtaining hope and joy in our personal lives is the reason we work so hard in our professional lives. One symbiotically feeds the other. We are to take joy in our work.

Solomon, reportedly the wisest man who ever lived, pondered the meaning of life. He concluded, "I have seen the business that God has given to the children of man . . . I perceived that there is nothing better for them than to be joyful and to do good as long as they live; also that everyone should eat and drink and take pleasure in all his toil—this is God's gift to man" (Ecclesiastes 3:10–13). We are to take joy in our labor! "There is nothing better than that a man should rejoice in his work" (Ecclesiastes 3:22).

Cultivate hope as your companion in your professional and personal life. Hope's handmaiden is joy. Make the decision to intentionally enjoy God's blessings in the good times and the bad and rejoice over all God has provided for you. This joy will then become contagious and bring hope to those around you.

CONCLUSION

We all desire to thrive, but unfortunately, most of us have not developed the good habits and practices in our personal lives for long-term success. Often, as we focus on our careers, our personal lives and families become victims of our success. I encourage you to pursue the life-giving disciplines we discussed in this chapter: practicing humility, prioritizing a good marriage, pursuing abundance and generosity, developing contentment, accepting correction, and cultivating hope and joy.

KEY ACTION ITEMS

1. **Practice Humility**—Don't believe your own press that you are God's gift to project management. Seek to have the right opinion of yourself—not too high and not too low. Realize that you can

always learn from others. Seek counsel and be deliberate when making decisions. Embrace humility as a lifelong goal.

2. **Prioritize a Good Marriage**—Good marriages are a treasure for life. They are a source of joy, strength, confidence, encouragement, and companionship. Invest in your marriage by intentionally planning and coordinating your calendars for vacations, walks, and dates. Try to emotionally connect with each other for at least five minutes every day. Avoid the snare of infidelity by establishing a good offense and "enjoying the wife of your youth."

3. **Pursue Abundance and Generosity**—Don't have a mindset of scarcity where there are only so many pieces of pie to go around. Live a life of abundance by being generous to others with your time and resources. Give freely to charities and the poor, and remember: "One who waters will himself be watered" (Proverbs 11:25). There is no quick path to wealth. Be "slow and steady" as you live below your means so you can be generous to others.

4. **Develop Contentment**—Seek to be at peace and content in all circumstances. A life well lived produces contentment. Have the strength to be kind to others without seeking favors in return. Lower your bar for accumulating wealth, and give thanks to God that you have a roof over your head, food on your plate, socks on your feet, and a bed to sleep in. Acknowledge that, in the end, everything good in your life is a gift from God.

5. **Accept Correction**—The path to thriving in life requires making course corrections along the way. Surround yourself with a group of colleagues and friends who promise to speak to you honestly about your life. Realize it will not necessarily be pleasant. We all need honest feedback and, at times, correction. Be willing to learn and adjust course.

6. **Cultivate Hope and Joy**—Joy is the fruit of hope and a life well lived. Develop hope by *looking* forward, not just moving forward. Choose joy! Intentionally find joy in the work of your hands and in your family and community. Invite hope to be your companion as you walk the path of life.

CHAPTER 10

INSTRUCTIONS TO YOUR HEART

Keep your heart with all vigilance, for from it flow the springs of life.

PROVERBS 4:23

While working on a large, complex project overrun with problems, I reached a point of crisis. I didn't have allies, and every day I spent 60 percent of my time in conflict with the client, my joint-venture partners, and my own executives—while still trying to build the project. I was ready to quit and angrily tell people what I thought of them on the way out the door! Mentally and emotionally, I was not in a good place. What was I to do when I couldn't think my way out of my anger and discouragement? I felt alone and abandoned, and I didn't want to repeat my bad habit of banging my head against the wall, pushing through the dysfunction to complete a project, and ending up in the hospital again.

It is exactly at these most stressful times that we need soul care—to quiet the chaos so we can discern our hearts and find the best path forward. My feelings of frustration were valid, but my resentment was clouding my thinking. I needed to slow down and allow time to process and gain clarity.

Ancient texts assert that understanding comes from our spirit: "For who knows a person's thoughts except the spirit of that person, which is in him?" (1 Corinthians 2:11). The human being's spirit, or heart, is an essential source of insight into our inner self. It enables us to reflect upon ideas, discern thoughts, and evaluate actions.

The word *heart*, used throughout Proverbs and Psalms, means the totality of a human's inner or immaterial nature. It refers to the "three traditional personality functions of man: emotion, thought or will."[16] We are more than physical beings; we are spiritual beings. King Solomon wrote, "[God] has made everything beautiful in its time . . . he has put eternity into man's heart" (Ecclesiastes 3:11). We are eternal beings who have deep-rooted longings we do not fully understand. In rare moments, we get a taste of the transcendent as we witness a gorgeous sunset, hear a haunting melody, gaze up at a night sky filled with stars, or view a completely still mountain lake. Perhaps it was watching your child be born that lifted your heart, or mourning a loved one that gave you a hunger for something more.

We often sense there is something beyond this physical world, but many of us are not in touch with our hearts. We can easily neglect our hearts when we're busy with work, family, entertainment, and the worries of life. Sometimes we intentionally keep ourselves busy to avoid reflecting on the most important aspects of life. When we fail to acknowledge or nurture the spiritual part of who we are, our lives will not be as rich and meaningful as they're meant to be.

> **WE OFTEN SENSE THERE IS SOMETHING BEYOND THIS PHYSICAL WORLD, BUT MANY OF US ARE NOT IN TOUCH WITH OUR HEARTS.**

During my time of doubt, distress, and resentment, I needed to slow down, take walks, pray, read sacred texts, journal, and seek counsel from my wife, God, and spiritual mentors. I had to give space to my spiritual life so I could properly decide on the right path forward. If I had relied only on my emotions and my mind, I would have confidently moved forward in the wrong direction. The time I spent instructing my heart gave me hope and encouraged me to continue to lead the project unencumbered by lack of support.

In this chapter, we will discuss the consequences of neglecting our hearts. Next, we will explore the starting place for attending to your heart, which is God's posture toward you. Finally, we will look at six simple, practical ways to develop a spiritual life.

CONSEQUENCES OF NEGLECTING YOUR HEART

Today, the mental health profession is reeling from the number of people suffering from anxiety, depression, addiction, and a general loss of hope and purpose. According to the US Food and Drug Administration, over 40 million Americans have been diagnosed with an anxiety disorder.[17] The pandemic opened a floodgate to anxiety and panic attacks, and this surge has not stopped since the pandemic officially ended.

According to the American Psychological Association, nearly three in five people say they feel mentally and emotionally exhausted. This striking phenomenon has been termed the "other" pandemic.[18]

Growing concerns around the dangers of loneliness prompted a call to action by former US Surgeon General Vivek Murthy, who released an eighty-two-page advisory on the issue.[19] The advisory cites data from several studies, including research that found nearly half of adults in the United States experience feelings of loneliness daily.[20]

Just as there are negative consequences for neglecting our physical health, there are consequences for neglecting our emotional and spiritual health. Not taking time to reflect and attend to our emotional and spiritual health leads to a lack of purpose and depression.

When we are out of touch with our hearts and living out of balance, we are more likely to struggle in our relationships with our spouse, our family, and those important to us. These stressful relationships often lead to guilt and a sense of regret. In some circumstances, guilt can be productive, inspiring us to acknowledge our own failings, which leads to forgiveness and reconciliation. But if guilt is left unaddressed, it can cause emotional and mental distress.

Proverbs 27:19 states, "As in water face reflects face, so the heart of man reflects the man." Your heart or soul is a true sign of how you are doing and who you are. Recognize the symptoms of neglecting your soul. When the psalmist struggled with depression and loneliness, he understood what he needed: "O God, you are my God; earnestly I seek you; my soul thirsts for you; my flesh faints for you, as in a dry and weary land where there is no water" (Psalm 63:1).

GOD'S POSTURE TOWARD YOU

I awoke one morning dreading a tough meeting where complaints (some valid and some not) were going to be leveled at me. So, before going to the meeting, I took time to quiet my heart before God. I prayed and thought about how I wanted to respond to whatever criticism I faced. As I read scripture, I was struck by the Apostle Paul's exhortation to "Outdo one another in showing honor" (Romans 12:10). I brought that attitude to the meeting, and I was able to graciously listen, respond, and clarify misunderstandings. If I hadn't taken the time to quiet my soul and rest in God's presence, I would have gone into the meeting defensive, angry, and unwilling to receive any correction. Frankly, I would have damaged valuable long-term relationships.

How do you prepare for meetings you know will be full of conflict and accusations? Do you ever turn toward God when you need help? The psalmist writes, "The Lord is near to all who call on him, to all who call on him in truth. He fulfills the desire of those who fear him; he also hears their cry and saves them" (Psalm 145:18–19). God is not hiding in the universe waiting to be found. He is nearby. Several times in Psalms, the writers paint a beautiful

> **GOD IS NOT HIDING IN THE UNIVERSE WAITING TO BE FOUND. HE IS NEARBY.**

picture of God leaning toward us with his ear ready to hear our prayers in our time of need: "I waited patiently for the Lord; he inclined to me and heard my cry" (Psalm 40:1). God's posture toward us is open and welcoming. He stands with his arms spread wide, waiting patiently for us to come to him and rest in his presence. He invites us to "draw near to the throne of grace, that we may receive mercy and find grace to help in time of need" (Hebrews 4:16).

When God proclaimed who he was to Moses, he stated, "The Lord, the Lord, a God merciful and gracious, slow to anger, and abounding in steadfast love and faithfulness, keeping steadfast love for thousands, forgiving iniquity and transgression and sin" (Exodus 34:6–7). We can take comfort that God does not greet us with anger when we come to him but with love, patience, faithfulness, graciousness, mercy, and forgiveness. That is why the prophet Joel, who lived about five hundred years before Jesus, exhorts us, "Return to the Lord your God, for he is gracious and merciful, slow to anger, and abounding in steadfast love" (Joel 2:13).

God is not waiting for your self-reformation or six-month training plan to be a better person; he welcomes you into his presence now. The Bible says, "Draw near to God, and he will draw near to you" (James 4:8). God promises renewal and rest when we come to him just as we are.

During Covid, my daughter's life was turned upside down.[21] Her college campus closed, all her classes went online, and she moved home for a year. Taken out of her community and away from supportive friends, she struggled with anxiety and depression. How was she to get back on track?

Fortunately, she had an opportunity to sign up for a class on spiritual practices as an elective for her major. This class encouraged her to lean into her spiritual life. She created an intentional space to help her body and mind slow down and be spiritually present. She also scheduled times throughout the week to attend to her heart.

You, too, can create space and time to develop a spiritual life by making little tweaks and changes in your daily schedule. You don't need to cut yourself off completely from the world, like a monk or nun. Simply carve out times in your week to take a break from the busyness and demands of life. As my daughter discovered, taking time to develop a spiritual life actually enhances your enjoyment of the world.

> **TAKING TIME TO DEVELOP A SPIRITUAL LIFE ACTUALLY ENHANCES YOUR ENJOYMENT OF THE WORLD.**

SIX SIMPLE AND PRACTICAL WAYS TO DEVELOP A SPIRITUAL LIFE

Read Sacred Texts—As I mentioned in an earlier chapter, I have developed the habit of reading five Psalms and one Proverb each day. On the one-year anniversary of my prostate surgery, I happened to read Psalm 103, and I was struck by verses two and three: "Bless the Lord, O my soul . . . who heals all your diseases." It was deeply meaningful to be reminded that it is God who sees my needs and heals me, that through competent doctors and God's healing grace, I was now cancer-free.

Stopping and giving thanks to God is good for our souls. Intentionally being thankful, even in sickness, is part of leading an abundant life. Creating the space to nurture our spiritual lives through reading sacred texts gives us the right perspective to live a life of peace and joy.

To develop a spiritual life, I suggest you begin with a goal of reading sacred texts for five minutes each day. You can learn a lot in five minutes. When I am running late and want to get on the road to avoid traffic, I'll just read one chapter in the Bible or listen to an audio Bible while driving to the project.

If you don't know where to start, I suggest reading Proverbs, Psalms, or the Gospel of John. There are Bible apps you can use, [22] and you can also find simple reading plans online—*The One Year Bible*, *The Chronological Bible*, *Daily Light*, *Our Daily Bread*, and many others. Peppered throughout this book are verses from Proverbs and Psalms that have inspired me and fed my soul. I have compiled these and other verses on my website (SchraederSolutions.com) to download so you can easily reference them by topic.

Pray—Prayer is simply talking to God. There are many different traditions and rituals for prayer, but don't overthink it or worry about doing it wrong. Just tell God what is on your mind. In his book *SoulShaping*, Douglas Rumford has a wonderful tip on prayer that he calls Preview.[23] Doug suggests that at the start of each day, you review your calendar and ask God to show up and help you in each meeting or situation. Then, at the end of the day, he suggests you do a Review[24]

> **PRAYER IS SIMPLY TALKING TO GOD.**

and reflect on how God met you that day. These simple prayers alert you to God's presence in your life.

Psalm 107:8–9 states, "Let them thank the Lord for his steadfast love, for his wondrous works to the children of man! For he satisfies the longing soul, and the hungry soul he fills with good things." Note that it is God who satisfies the longing in your soul and fills you with good things. Therefore, thank him when you pray—for how he met you through the day and for the good things in your life. This leads to contentment.

And don't forget to tell God about concerns you have for yourself, your friends, and your family. Every night, my wife and I pray for our three children and their spouses and for any issues we or our friends or extended family are facing. These types of prayers are modeled for us in Psalms: "Give ear, O Lord, to my prayer; And attend to the voice of my supplications. In the day of my trouble I will call upon You, For You will answer me" (Psalm 86:6–7, NKJV).

During the Covid lockdowns in the spring of 2020, my wife and I had extra time on our hands because almost every store, restaurant, and public space was closed. We used this time and slower pace for more self-reflection and assessment. We would take long walks to our local park, sit on a bench, and watch the geese and ducks making perfect Vs in the water, their goslings and ducklings swimming behind them. We would talk and pray about concerns we had and where we were stuck and needed help moving on. I treasure this sacred time and the resulting emotional healing and well-being it brought.

You can begin by simply talking to God each day. Tell him what is on your heart. Ask him to show you who he is and what he asks of you. Ask God to show you who *you* are and how you can be a better spouse, friend, parent, and project manager.

Meditate and Journal—As project managers, our minds are extremely busy and full of tasks we must do or should have done or need to schedule to do. We rarely leave any time in our daily calendars to think and process. We fill any free time we have with family responsibilities, well-earned fun activities, exercise, and entertainment. The thought of slowing down enough to meditate and journal is foreign to most of us.

The original word ancients used for meditating means to mutter, moan, or growl. It was an inarticulate sound like a dove cooing or a lion growling over prey.[25] My dad was an incredibly talented carpenter, and I remember hearing him mutter to himself as he framed a house. Under his breath, he would say, "Gonna frame this corner, see she's four-square, straight and plumb. Then square up this wall . . ." And he would go on uttering unintelligible phrases till he finished the job.

In a similar way, meditating is muttering thoughts around a problem, a question, or a truth to be applied or understood. Many times we are awakened at night by our subconscious mind actively trying to solve the problems of the day. When this happens to me, the only way I can get back to sleep is to mutter to God about the issue and give it to him. The psalmist writes, "My soul will be satisfied as with fat and rich food, and my mouth will praise you with joyful lips, when I remember you upon my bed, and meditate on you in the watches of the night" (Psalm 63:5–6). I am comforted to know that I am not alone. Over three thousand years ago, wise men and women were waking up at night thinking about problems and meditating on God.

Psalm 77 is a great example of meditation. The writer begins with an honest expression of what he's feeling: "When I remember God, I moan; when I meditate, my spirit faints" (vs. 3). He determines to set his thoughts on God and reflect on his own life: "I said, 'Let me remember my song in the night; let me meditate in my heart.' Then my spirit made a diligent search" (vs. 6). He asks many questions about the character of God and recites God's past faithfulness: "I will ponder all your work, and meditate on your mighty deeds" (vs. 12). In the midst of his struggles, the psalmist's meditation eventually leads his heart to a place of peace and confidence.

When you meditate, it's a great idea to write down your thoughts. You can write what you are learning, what you are struggling with, or even prayers. You can choose to write advice to yourself by imagining your future self in ten years and telling yourself how to stay on track. You can complain about people who are irritating you. You can do as the psalmist did and write down questions you are struggling with and then wait for God to answer. Journaling helps focus your mind.

I don't like writing in a physical journal. I use my iPad with a keyboard to record struggles I'm having or epiphanies that come to me while meditating. This allows me to share my notes with my wife. If you prefer using pen and paper, buy a nice journal to record your thoughts. Whatever type of journal you choose, write down your questions, struggles, insights, and prayers. After a month, read back over them. You will be surprised by the clarity and peace gained from meditating and journaling.

Wait on God—In our fast-paced lives, the last thing we want to do is wait. I'm always amazed when I see cars lined up in drive-throughs to get coffee or fast food. I hate waiting in long lines, especially at airports. But ancient wisdom informs us to wait on the Lord. The psalmist writes, "For God alone my soul waits in silence; from him comes my salvation. He alone is my rock and my salvation, my fortress; I shall not be greatly shaken" (Psalm 62:1–2).

Several years ago, I had a big career decision to make, and I didn't have clarity. My family and I were on vacation in Europe staying with some friends at a working farm just outside of Salzburg. Most of the group planned to drive to a nearby village for the day, but I decided to stay behind and wait on God. I took a journal, hiked up the hill behind the farm, and sat on a log with a beautiful view of the valley and the Alps. I still distinctly remember the striking view, the lush colors of the trees, the fresh smell of the mountain air, and the quiet of the forest. In that beautiful space, I wrote down the pros and cons of the potential career change and gave God the decision. Then I waited until I had some inkling of his confirmation. Waiting on God gave me the confidence to move forward with a big decision that was greatly beneficial to my career.

When our lives are going well, we often don't turn to God or wait on him. During health scares, tragedies, broken family relationships, or great disappointments in our careers, we may turn to God and ask, "What are you doing?" When I was ill with viral encephalitis, I had no choice but to slow down and reflect on how I had become sick as I waited to gain full strength, which took almost a year. As I recovered and waited on God, I was encouraged. As the ancients advise, "Wait for the Lord; be strong, and let your heart take courage; wait for the Lord!" (Psalm 27:14).

Three times in my life I have been devastated by betrayals at work. I still vividly remember the feelings of abandonment and hopelessness. In those situations, I had no choice but to turn to God and wait patiently for him. I didn't know it at the time, but in each of these situations, God was moving me away from a dysfunctional team to better opportunities. With the perspective of time, I can now see that what I thought was bad was actually for my good.

Waiting on God is instructive to your heart. As you wait, you give God everything that is troubling you and rest in his goodness, mercy, and grace. Waiting is being still, seeking solitude, and listening. Simply ask God to meet you and provide his peace and direction. Then wait for his peace before moving forward.

> SIMPLY ASK GOD TO MEET YOU AND PROVIDE HIS PEACE AND DIRECTION.

Live in Community and Serve—In the West, we are highly individualistic and don't often value community. The last thing we want to do is be directed or controlled by family, work, government, or faith communities. It is part of our culture to be independent—masters of our own destiny. In contrast, people in Africa, South America, the Middle East, and other parts of the world are much more group oriented and greatly value their families and tribes. An African proverb illustrates this: "If you want to go fast, go alone. If you want to go far, go together."[26] To go far, we need other people with collective experiences who can feed into our lives and hearts. As the ancients inform us, "Iron sharpens iron, and one man sharpens another" (Proverbs 27:17).

To find this community, join a church or another faith group. It is good for our hearts to be around others who are intentionally nurturing their spiritual lives and can point out path corrections when we wander. It is also good for our families. My wife and I fondly remember the many pool parties we hosted for families at our church. At the time, our children were of the age where cooler parents had more clout than we did. (Somehow, when our children became teenagers, my wife and I became less cool and intelligent.) This community of families provided other adults who modeled wise life choices and spoke truth into our children's lives, which helped them mature into responsible adults with good values.

Living in community also encourages a healthy life balance. As leaders with challenging jobs, we need to be able to commiserate with others about our demanding schedules and discuss how we can do our job and still build into our marriages, families, and communities. Seeing friends set priorities in their schedule to spend time with their families and not let work take over their lives encouraged me to do the same. We all need encouragement to make the right choices that are good for our souls. The benefit of living in community is when we see others making good decisions, we are motivated to do the same.

> **WE ALL NEED ENCOURAGEMENT TO MAKE THE RIGHT CHOICES THAT ARE GOOD FOR OUR SOULS.**

Living in community also exposes us to those less fortunate than we are and gives us opportunities to help others. Our church has a transitional living home for recovering drug addicts and homeless men, helping them rebuild their lives physically and spiritually. It usually takes at least eighteen months for these men to reform their lives and get back on their feet. Every week, I have the joy of greeting these guys at church and acknowledging them as valuable members of our community as they turn their lives around.

Join a faith community, and you will be amazed at the lifelong benefits of living in relationship with others. Find out what you can do to serve those in your community. Your heart will be full as you share your life with others and see lives changed.

Forgive—The problem with living in community is that people will often offend and hurt us. This happens in all relationships, whether professional or personal. So, how do we guard our hearts from becoming bitter? Forgive. Doing the work of forgiveness is key to taking care of our hearts. Forgiveness is the antidote to bitterness, but forgiving others who have wronged us is difficult.

My wife has been a good partner in helping me forgive others. Recently, while resolving some tensions with a colleague, I was surprised when resentment surfaced about an incident that had occurred five years earlier. The intensity of my feelings alerted me that I needed to go back and forgive this individual who had wronged me. At first,

I was glib about it, but my wife encouraged me to revisit the incident and forgive the person for every word or action that hurt me. It was painful to walk through the troubling experience, but afterward the resentment lifted, and I felt lighter and ready to move forward.

You don't need to wait for someone to ask for forgiveness before forgiving them. And forgiveness does not mean reconciliation. Forgiveness is releasing the pain of being wronged and giving the person to God. Forgiveness cuts out the growing root of bitterness that can poison your whole life.

There are also times when we need to request forgiveness from God. The Apostle John writes, "If we confess our sins, he is faithful and just to forgive us our sins and to cleanse us from all unrighteousness" (1 John 1:9). Never be afraid to go to God and ask for forgiveness. Or to ask forgiveness from those you may have intentionally or unintentionally wronged. I cannot overstate how sweet it is to forgive and to be forgiven.

THE REST OF THE STORY

I would like to finish my daughter's story. When she intentionally nurtured her spiritual life, she didn't do it perfectly. She says it was messy, and she had to recognize her initial state of being distracted and self-condemning. To help her focus, she wrote down or spoke her struggles aloud, which allowed her to let down her guard and be still and hear from God. She says the transformative result was having more grace with herself. Taken out of the routine of daily life and having the space to process the things of her heart, she was reminded of God's goodness and grace in her life so she could then show herself grace. In slowing down, she learned to question the source of different negative thoughts: *Is that thought true, or is it a lie I believe about myself? Have some family or friends made judgments on me that aren't true?*

At the end of this period of nurturing her spiritual life, the primary message she heard from God was, "Rest and trust me." This was transformative and helped her overcome her anxieties and depression and move into a healthier and more productive stage of life.

Consider the six simple steps to develop a spiritual life: read sacred texts, pray, meditate and journal, wait on God, live in community and serve, and forgive. Slowly develop your spiritual muscles, and as they grow, your desire to instruct your heart will increase. As my daughter experienced, developing a spiritual life makes you aware of God's presence and helps you become a person of confidence and compassion. Attending to your heart brings peace and joy to your conflict-filled, fast-paced life and provides balance in the demanding world of project management. It also leads to an abundant life as you become fully present in all you do, without focusing on past regrets or worries about the future.

CONCLUSION

By no means do I claim to be an expert at attending to my heart. I am a fellow traveler who regularly makes wrong judgments about myself, others, and God. Out of those judgments come debilitating vows and potential bitterness through lack of forgiveness and holding on to how I've been wronged. I must daily quiet my heart and go before God. When I listen, pray, read, and meditate, I obtain a correct view of myself, God, and others, and I feel lighter and strengthened to tackle the challenges of each day.

The psalmist wrote, "He satisfies the longing soul, and the hungry soul he fills with good things" (Psalm 107:9). God is the one who satisfies the longing of our souls. He provides purpose, heals our hearts, and meets our eternal longings. A quote credited to Blaise Pascal, the famous mathematician and astronomer, says it well: "There is a God-shaped vacuum in the heart of every man which cannot be filled by any created thing, but only by God, the Creator, made known through Jesus."

A vibrant spiritual life doesn't happen on its own. Like anything worthwhile, you must put work into the development of your heart.

True growth happens when a vision for a better life captivates you, and you commit to take the steps necessary to nurture a more abundant life. Caring for your heart is critical to living a life of wisdom. The ancients knew this and exhorted, "Keep your heart with all vigilance, for from it flow the springs of life" (Proverbs 4:23).

> **TRUE GROWTH HAPPENS WHEN A VISION FOR A BETTER LIFE CAPTIVATES YOU.**

KEY ACTION ITEMS

1. **Acknowledge Your Heart**—You are more than just a physical and mental being. Eternity has been placed in your heart. Acknowledge this truth and make plans to care for your soul to live a productive life of joy and peace.

2. **Consequences of Neglecting Your Heart**—Anxiety, depression, lack of purpose, loneliness, and unresolved guilt from broken relationships are symptoms of not caring for your heart. Recognize the symptoms in your life that instruct you to invest in your spiritual life.

3. **God's Posture Toward You**—God is nearby. He welcomes you into his presence. He does not require self-reformation before he meets with you. Go to God to rest in his care as you develop your spiritual life and instruct your heart. He is the one pursuing you and welcomes you with open arms.

4. **Six Simple and Practical Ways to Develop a Spiritual Life**—Plan your daily schedule to include activities to nurture a spiritual life. Read the Bible or other sacred texts for five minutes a day. Pray by simply talking to God throughout your day. Meditate and journal about your struggles and what you are learning. Plan times to slow your pace of life so you can wait and listen to God. Choose a faith community to be involved with and surround yourself with like-minded people. Finally, do the work of forgiveness to avoid resentment and bitterness in your life.

APPENDIX

SUMMARY OF ACTION ITEMS

CHAPTER 2—EXCEL IN TECHNICAL ACUMEN

KEY ACTION ITEMS

1. **Humbly Pursue Knowledge and Technical Excellence**—Ask questions, be observant, and ask your technical experts and mentors what they would do. Take notes, write out a project management plan, and have other managers review it. Never be afraid to admit what you don't know—this is the beginning of wisdom.

2. **Identify the Industry Standards for Your Project**—What does your client or owner specify? What do they use as a resource? What do your mentors use for standards? Assemble a list of design criteria and specifications that define success for the project. If they do not exist, write them up and show them to your client.

3. **Define Your Project and Scope**—What is the scope of work, and what are the design criteria and specifications? What are your source documents? How do you separate opinions from facts? What is your project? How do you know when you're done? What does success look like in this project?

4. **Develop Mentors**—Make a list of technical, managerial, and financial areas in which you are deficient. Identify two experienced professionals for each of these areas and ask them to be your mentor. The one mentor you *must* have is the one who will teach you the difference between cost and revenue in project management.

5. **Move Forward Confidently**—You have what it takes to be successful. Put your head down and work without complaining. All the technical expertise you obtain will be part of you for the rest of your career.

CHAPTER 3—LEAD YOUR TEAM

KEY ACTION ITEMS

1. **Define Your Organizational Chart and Direct Reports**—Determine the size of your team by evaluating how many people it takes to complete your project in the time allotted. Divide up the work based on the anticipated burn rate and technical discipline leads in your industry. Then determine your direct reports (no more than five) based on the critical path or greatest risk to manage the project successfully.

2. **Delegate Properly**—Give your direct reports the authority and responsibility to complete their tasks. Hold them accountable for their action items. Make sure they leave meetings with the monkey on their back and that you don't take on their tasks.

3. **Recruit the Right People**—Be quick to fire and slow to hire. Put time into recruiting and hiring the right people with a defined process of interviews and questions that get at the core of who people are and how they will perform under stress.

4. **Make Good Decisions**—Do not strive to be the smartest person in the room. Model open discussion until you can arrive at the right path forward with input from your team. Ask good questions to solicit honest feedback. Most of your managers don't have the confidence to tell you when you are wrong.

5. **Celebrate and Encourage**—Make your project the most desired project to work on by celebrating your team's victories. Plan these celebrations to build team relationships and reward those who are excelling. Put together a short-term and long-term incentive plan

and communicate it. Say "Thank you" and "Good job!" Positive acknowledgment often leads to higher employee satisfaction than more remuneration.

CHAPTER 4—PROTECT YOUR SCOPE AND MARGIN

KEY ACTION ITEMS

1. **Anticipate Scope Creep and Delays**—If you are managing a project, the client or their representatives will want you to add scope and do it for free. Don't be surprised at this request. Expect it and plan for it. Be emotionally and organizationally prepared to provide a written notice of a potential increase in costs due to an increase in the scope of work.

2. **Provide Timely Notice**—Assign a manager to be responsible for making all written notices required by your contract. Use the vast experience of your team and discipline managers to email the claims manager on notices that need to be sent out. Authorize your field leads to email notice of changes in field conditions to the owner's representatives. Remember that you are being kind to provide timely notice in compliance with the contract to allow your client to reduce cost and schedule impacts.

3. **Prepare for Conflict**—Prepare your project management organization (estimator, scheduler, cost engineer) to deal with change orders and recovery. Assign an administrative assistant under your contracts manager to prepare a bookmarked document of all correspondence (organized by date). Do not antagonize your client in your correspondence and communications. Stay professional and courteous. Bring your client into the strategy of mitigating delays and completing the project on time.

4. **Strategize to Win**—Realize that you are not God's gift to change management. Get input and critiques from senior managers and lawyers (if necessary) on your merit argument. Assign senior key

leaders or construction lawyers to prepare your claims. Plan for arbitration with the right level of protection for your key experts. Do not abdicate leadership. Stay involved and lead!

CHAPTER 5—RELATIONSHIPS ARE YOUR BIGGEST ASSET

KEY ACTION ITEMS

1. **Genuinely Love People**—Are you demonstrating your love for others by wanting what is best for them in their careers and personal lives? Be kind for the sake of being kind. Especially show kindness to those below you in the org chart and the administrative gatekeepers to your clients. Empathize with others and realize your client and team have problems outside of work that impact the project.

2. **Build Effective Relationships**—Build relationships by applying the Golden Rule, treating others—employees, clients, and executives—how you want to be treated. Calendarize lunches and time for unofficial business visits. Play sports together if you can. If you don't play sports, plan to attend an event together outside of work. Make deposits of trust in your relationships. Stay in relationship with difficult subs and vendors by being professional and making timely payments.

3. **Be a Person of Peace**—Become that person others want to come and talk to. Be a safe person by controlling your anger. Strive to be approachable by keeping your door open to talk with people and speak gracious words. Be winsome and friendly. Be someone others actually enjoy being with and working with, even when you're solving problems together. Become a confidant to your client and teammates. Provide earnest counsel and receive it from friends who care about you.

4. **Create Joy**—Finally, create joy in your project. Joy and leadership start at the top. You have a tremendous opportunity to lead and

help make others successful as you build projects that you could never accomplish on your own. Make your project joyful!

CHAPTER 6—KNOW HOW TO NEGOTIATE

KEY ACTION ITEMS

1. **Recognize Your Default Conflict Mode in Negotiations**—Are you *competing, accommodating, avoiding, collaborating*, or *compromising*? Are you trying to preserve relationships and avoid conflict, or are you putting all your energy into accomplishing your goals regardless of others? There is no wrong answer, but do a self-evaluation and shore up your negotiations with team members of different strengths.

2. **Practice Prudence and Discretion**—All negotiation tactics and planning can be reduced to prudence and discretion. Discretion is staying quiet and listening. Prudence is saying the right thing at the right time to the right audience. The ancients knew that this was the essence of wisdom: "I, wisdom, dwell with prudence, and I find knowledge and discretion" (Proverbs 8:12). The only way to be prudent and stay quiet is to prepare for negotiations.

3. **Plan Your Steps**—You will not have successful negotiations if you do not take the time to plan. Prepare for negotiations by gathering your team, identifying your goals (financial and contractual), preparing emotionally to engage in negotiations, and scripting your qualitative questions. Write on one sheet of paper your high goal, the makeup of your team, your strengths in merit, and the open-ended qualitative questions (How? What? When?).

4. **Negotiate With Confidence**—There are multiple tactics and strategies to negotiating. First, don't do it alone—bring a team to listen and learn during negotiations. Always let the other side go first. Stay flexible and slow down the negotiations so you can learn what the real issues are to reaching a settlement. Embrace the

strong "no" that comes from the other side of the table. You are now close to reaching a deal. Close the deal by letting your client state the settlement amount first. They will then be committed to shepherding the settlement through to the end.

5. **Finally, a Warning**—Don't demand justice because you have been financially damaged by your client or their representatives. If you show anger early on in negotiations, you will fail. You may be completely contractually correct in your position, but at the end of the day, realize your goal is to successfully close out your negotiations and move on to the next job. Remember to be persuasive and not angry. "The heart of the wise makes his speech judicious and adds persuasiveness to his lips" (Proverbs 16:23).

CHAPTER 7—TRACK YOUR PERFORMANCE

KEY ACTION ITEMS

1. **Work Breakdown Structure (WBS)**—Delineate what detailed level of activities you want to roll up to your large headings or buckets of cost. Once you decide on these activities, set up cost codes and budgets for each one, then regularly review your costs. If your WBS is not sufficient to control your project, break it down into bite-sized pieces.

2. **Schedule**—Do not delegate your schedule to technicians. Be involved in setting up the schedule activities, logic ties, and sequence of work that defines your critical path. Understand and manage which activities can be completed concurrently and which are sequential. Review your monthly schedule updates to ensure they correctly define the critical path. Be careful not to create too many activities to track in your schedule.

3. **Costs**—Do not equate costs with revenue. Track your costs for the budgets you have set up for each item of work. Verify that your cost report is up to date with incurred costs (invoices, labor,

supplies, etc.). Do not succumb to the temptation to manipulate your cost report to avoid reporting bad results.

4. **Revenue**—Revenue is the value of your executed contract or purchase order. It is what you are paid monthly for your project. Track revenue to ensure you have more money coming in than going out. Have a defined process in place for recognizing soft revenue from claims or client-promised change orders. (I only recognize revenue with an executed change order.) Keep a separate risk/opportunity sheet to track potential future revenue.

5. **Reporting Estimated Cost at Completion**—Review your cost report and ECAC. Use the straight-line method of forecasting cost at completion based on unit cost of production occurring to date. Hold your discipline managers accountable for preparing their portion of the forecasts. Do not be overly optimistic in forecasting profit. Do not overpromise and underdeliver. Hold regular monthly and quarterly reviews.

6. **Cash Flow**—Cash is king! Be paid for the work you perform by setting up an accounts receivable process to send out notices and warnings of liens when not paid. Make a cash flow budget for your project before you start, and let executives know early if you need the company to finance your project with cash calls.

CHAPTER 8—BEWARE THE PITFALLS AND SNARES OF SUCCESS

KEY ACTION ITEMS

1. **The Slippery Path**—Pride is the lubricant on the path that leads to slipping and falling. Guard yourself from believing you are invulnerable and will never fail, or you can become entitled and think you deserve more for your work and leadership. Beware of the trap of pride and ego. Make sure you have people in your life who keep you accountable and give you honest feedback (friends, not fans).

2. **Destructive Sexual Relationships**—Many stronger and better people have fallen into this snare and destroyed their lives. Realize the great costs and consequences reckless sexual relationships will have on your family and reputation. Know that you are susceptible to this trap, and develop a good defense to avoid it. Do not place yourself alone, with alcohol and weariness, in a potentially dangerous situation. Practice the "Irish goodbye" and just walk away.

3. **Avarice**—Don't let greed and the pursuit of wealth steal your life. Wealth is fleeting. We all know people who have lost money, but we don't think it will apply to us. Realize that fear of scarcity may drive your decisions. Choose to live below your means, be content, and invest relationally in your family, who will carry on your legacy after you are gone.

4. **Lying and Fraud**—Fear and greed lead to lying and fraud. Beware that this begins with small lies and fudges that can develop into fraud that could put you in jail. Don't start down the path of willfully adjusting your financial reporting. There is no better defense than the truth. When there are financial problems, come clean right away and then try to recover the losses.

5. **Self-Medication and Addictions**—Beware of self-medicating your pain and stress with alcohol and drugs. This only provides temporary relief and can lead to an early death. Depressants (alcohol), hallucinogens (LSD, marijuana), and stimulants (crystal meth) all cause massive health problems and can lead to long-term mental health issues. Recognize the symptoms of addiction early and get help through counseling and a twelve-step program.

6. **Anger, Bitterness, and Envy**—Don't be discontented and poison yourself with anger, bitterness, and envy. Do regular emotional check-ins on yourself. Ask your spouse and/or good friends for feedback. Take responsibility for your emotional health.

CHAPTER 9—CREATE LONG-TERM SUCCESS

KEY ACTION ITEMS

1. **Practice Humility**—Don't believe your own press that you are God's gift to project management. Seek to have the right opinion of yourself—not too high and not too low. Realize that you can always learn from others. Seek counsel and be deliberate when making decisions. Embrace humility as a lifelong goal.

2. **Prioritize a Good Marriage**—Good marriages are a treasure for life. They are a source of joy, strength, confidence, encouragement, and companionship. Invest in your marriage by intentionally planning and coordinating your calendars for vacations, walks, and dates. Try to emotionally connect with each other for at least five minutes every day. Avoid the snare of infidelity by establishing a good offense and "enjoying the wife of your youth."

3. **Pursue Abundance and Generosity**—Don't have a mindset of scarcity where there are only so many pieces of pie to go around. Live a life of abundance by being generous to others with your time and resources. Give freely to charities and the poor, and remember: "One who waters will himself be watered" (Proverbs 11:25). There is no quick path to wealth. Be "slow and steady" as you live below your means so you can be generous to others.

4. **Develop Contentment**—Seek to be at peace and content in all circumstances. A life well lived produces contentment. Have the strength to be kind to others without seeking favors in return. Lower your bar for accumulating wealth, and give thanks to God that you have a roof over your head, food on your plate, socks on your feet, and a bed to sleep in. Acknowledge that, in the end, everything good in your life is a gift from God.

5. **Accept Correction**—The path to thriving in life requires making course corrections along the way. Surround yourself with a group of colleagues and friends who promise to speak to you honestly

about your life. Realize it will not necessarily be pleasant. We all need honest feedback and, at times, correction. Be willing to learn and adjust course.

6. **Cultivate Hope and Joy**—Joy is the fruit of hope and a life well lived. Develop hope by *looking* forward, not just moving forward. Choose joy! Intentionally find joy in the work of your hands and in your family and community. Invite hope to be your companion as you walk the path of life.

CHAPTER 10—INSTRUCTIONS TO YOUR HEART

KEY ACTION ITEMS

1. **Acknowledge Your Heart**—You are more than just a physical and mental being. Eternity has been placed in your heart. Acknowledge this truth and make plans to care for your soul to live a productive life of joy and peace.

2. **Consequences of Neglecting Your Heart**—Anxiety, depression, lack of purpose, loneliness, and unresolved guilt from broken relationships are symptoms of not caring for your heart. Recognize the symptoms in your life that instruct you to invest in your spiritual life.

3. **God's Posture Toward You**—God is nearby. He welcomes you into his presence. He does not require self-reformation before he meets with you. Go to God to rest in his care as you develop your spiritual life and instruct your heart. He is the one pursuing you and welcomes you with open arms.

4. **Six Simple and Practical Ways to Develop a Spiritual Life**—Plan your daily schedule to include activities to nurture a spiritual life. Read the Bible or other sacred texts five minutes a day. Pray by simply talking to God throughout your day. Meditate and journal about your struggles and what you are learning. Plan times to slow your pace of life so you can wait and listen to God. Choose a

faith community to be involved with and surround yourself with like-minded people. Finally, do the work of forgiveness to avoid resentment and bitterness in your life.

ACKNOWLEDGMENTS

Writing a book is a much larger task than I had imagined. I didn't wake up one day with the skills and knowledge to write a book. Many people have graciously invested in my life, and I am thankful for their gift of time and knowledge.

My father instilled in me a love of building and exhorted me at an early age to learn how to figure. I wouldn't have become a civil engineer and pursued design and construction without his influence.

My design mentors at RBF taught me the basics of horizontal control, roadway, grading, hydrology, water, sewer, and drainage design. I have taken these disciplines into every project.

My construction mentors taught me how to evaluate, price, and manage risk. Kent Reiman made sure I knew the difference between cost and revenue. Harry Young instructed me on how to manage claims. The incredible builders, superintendents, and construction engineers who figured out how to build the impossible—you are the reason I wrote this book. May you thrive in your professional and personal lives as you work in an extraordinary industry.

Owners, clients, and their representatives—thank you for the opportunity to work on your projects. Even though at times we got sideways, together we persevered and built something remarkable we never could have done on our own.

To my Convene Peer Group—thank you for your input and encouragement. Special thanks to my Convene Leadership Coach, Paul Aubin, for his reviews and counsel.

To my wonderful children—thank you for allowing me to use your stories and insights in this book and for encouraging me to continue to make wise decisions in life so you always have a reason to be proud of your dad.

Finally, this book would not have been possible without the incredible assistance and support of my wonderful wife. Nancy, your excellence and persistence are an inspiration for me to become a better writer and a better partner in life.

"For the Lord gives wisdom; from his mouth come knowledge and understanding" (Proverbs 2:6). Thank you, Lord, for instructing me in the path of wisdom for "those who hold her fast are called blessed" (Proverbs 3:18).

LET'S CONNECT

For additional resources or to contact Robert for seminars, speaking, leadership coaching, or consulting, visit SchraederSolutions.com.

ABOUT THE AUTHOR

Robert Schraeder has managed projects totaling more than four billion dollars throughout his career. He is a leader in the construction and design industry and the former president of the American Society of Civil Engineers Construction Institute (ASCE CI). An industry executive and a licensed professional engineer, he is unique in project management, with experience both in design and construction. In addition to attaining bachelor of science degrees in civil engineering and applied mathematics, he earned a master of divinity from Talbot School of Theology and has been a lifelong learner, integrating biblical wisdom with leadership and managing projects. A gifted speaker and teacher, Robert is a professional leadership coach and the president of Schraeder Solutions.

ENDNOTES

1   Oncken, William Jr., and Donald L. Wass. "Management Time: Who's Got the Monkey." *Harvard Business Review*, November-December 1974, republished in November-December 1999.

2   Ibid., 6–7.

3   Del Sesto, Dean. Venthio Great Questions. www.venthio.com.

4   Lencioni, Patrick. *The Ideal Team Player*. San Francisco: Jossey-Bass, 2016.

5   *Merriam-Webster Dictionary*. s.v. empathy. https://www.merriam-webster.com/dictionary/empathy.

6   *Merriam-Webster Dictionary*. s.v. winsome. https://www.merriam-webster.com/dictionary/winsome.

7   *Convene*. convenenow.com.

8   Thomas, Kenneth. "Conflict and Conflict Management." *Handbook of Industrial and Organizational Psychology*, edited by Marvin Dunnette. Chicago: Rand McNally, 1976.

9   Ibid., 10.

10 "Thomas-Kilmann Instrument (TKI): 1 TKI per Person." *Kilmann Diagnostics*. 2009–2025. https://kilmanndiagnostics.com/assessments/thomas-kilmann-instrument-one-assessment-person/.

11 Voss, Chris, and Tahl Raz. *Never Split the Difference*. New York: HarperCollins, 2016.

12 Ibid., 35.

13 Ibid., 32.

14 Mikhail, Alexa. "Silicon Valley Elites Are Reportedly Taking Ketamine and Attending Psychedelic Parties to Bolster Their Focus and Creativity. Here's What the Drugs Do to Your Brain." *Fortune*, June 27, 2023. https://fortune.com/well/2023/06/27/silicon-valley-elites-ketamine-psychedelics-effects-on-brain/.

15 *Merriam-Webster Dictionary*. s.v. envy. https://www.merriam-webster.com/dictionary/envy.

16 Harris, R. Laird, Gleason L. Archer Jr., and Bruce K. Waltke. *Theological Wordbook of the Old Testament*. Chicago: Moody Press, 2003.

17 "Anxiety." *U.S. Food & Drug Administration*. Last modified July 10, 2024. https://www.fda.gov/consumers/health-education-resources/anxiety.

18 Breithaupt, Susan. "Exhaustion – The 'Other' Pandemic." *Valley Health System*. May 10, 2022. https://www.valleyhealth.com/trending/exhaustion-other-pandemic.

19 Murthy, Vivek H. MD. "Our Epidemic of Loneliness and Isolation." 2023. US Department of Health and Human Services. https://www.hhs.gov/sites/default/files/surgeon-general-social-connection-advisory.pdf.

20 Buechler, Jessica. "The Loneliness Epidemic Persists: A Post Pandemic Look at the State of Loneliness among U.S. Adults." *The Cigna Group*, 2021. https://newsroom.thecignagroup.com/all-stories?item=446.

21 I share this story with my daughter's permission.

22 Bible Hub, Blue Letter Bible, Holy Bible, ESV Bible, Bible Gateway, Logos Bible, Her Bible, and Dwell Audio Bible

23 Rumford, Douglas J. *SoulShaping*. Orange: Lorica Ministries, 2022.

24 Ibid., 110.

25 Brown, Francis, S.R. Driver, and Charles A. Briggs. *The Brown-Driver-Briggs Hebrew and English Lexicon*. Peabody: Hendrickson Publishers, 1996.

26 Rumford, Douglas J. *SoulShaping*. Orange: Lorica Ministries, 2022.

www.ingramcontent.com/pod-product-compliance
Lightning Source LLC
Chambersburg PA
CBHW031510120626
46545CB00005B/1820